Ed Oakley and Doug Krug

SIMON & SCHUSTER

NEW YORK   LONDON   TORONTO   SYDNEY   TOKYO   SINGAPORE

ENLIGHTENED LEADERSHIP

Getting to the Heart of Change

SIMON & SCHUSTER INC.
Simon & Schuster Building
Rockefeller Center
1230 Avenue of the Americas
New York, NY 10020

First Simon & Schuster Edition 1993

Published by arrangement with Key to Renewal, Inc.

Designed by Hyun Joo Kim
Manufactured in the United States of America

1   3   5   7   9   10   8   6   4   2

Library of Congress Cataloging-in-Publication Data is available.

ISBN: 0-671-86674-5

Edited by Nina Amir
Illustrations by Karen Saunders

This book is dedicated to our fathers,

Garland Lea Oakley (1918–89) and
Douglas Edward Krug (1917–80),

for their support, their challenges, and
their love.

ACKNOWLEDGMENTS

Because so many people have contributed to this book in different ways, it is very difficult to acknowledge only a few. This book truly represents the best we have been able to put into writing about what we have learned thus far through the experience of our lives. Thus, anyone who has contributed to our life experiences has contributed to this book.

Certainly, our families have contributed enormously in terms of support for our work, as well as the path of growth and maturation that we are on. It is your unconditional love, your total "partnership," and your total belief in us that continues to fuel us in our quest. We hope we have been able to express over the years the importance you have been and continue to be to us. In many ways, this book is as much yours as it is ours.

We would like to especially thank our "partners in renewal," our clients. Together, we have learned a lot about what it takes to bring out the best in people through Enlightened Leadership. Thank you for your continuing courage to step out and do what hasn't been done before. For your commitment to the truth. For your belief in the quest. For your dedication and belief in your people. For your ongoing openness to question the way it is, while on the path to discovering just how good it can be.

Our clients have urged us for years to write this book. Several of you, as well as other respected leaders, read the manuscript, and made recommendations which we feel resulted in a better book. Thank you for your encouragement and your commitment to the ongoing renewal of your people and your organizations.

We also want to thank those many people in organizations in which we were managers who so patiently endured our struggles of personal growth and personal leadership. When we discuss reactive leadership, we do so from a very intimate understanding of it! Thank you for hanging in there and teaching us many lessons.

There have been some special people in the consulting and writing arena that have been particularly influential to us over the years. Those who have had an inordinately valuable impact on us include Larry Miller, Pete Block, Larry Wilson, Stephen Covey, Kurt and Patricia Wright, Tom Peters, Juanell Teague and Perry Pascarella. Several you will recognize as accomplished authors. Thanks each of you for *your* work that has contributed so greatly to our understanding of what it takes to bring out the best in people.

Then there are those who most directly worked on the book. Our primary editor was Nina Amir, who rightfully challenged us to rewrite over and over until this book was readable! Thank you, Nina, for your persistence and the quality which resulted. For all the time and effort you have put into bringing this dream to reality, thank you Suzanne Newman. Thank you for being true to yourself and for the courage to support us in being true to ourselves. And a very special thanks to Dianne Baker, who had the courage to tell us when the book was not ready. Her contributions were instrumental in making the book what it is today.

For providing editorial suggestions and performing numerous proofreading chores, we thank our friends Joe Sabah, LaDawn Westbrook, and Therese Krug. Your contributions were vital to us.

In addition to her own editing, proofreading and indexing contributions, Carol Dovi impressively coordinated the massive and complex job of managing two "writers" and the myriad of pieces that had to come together to make this book possible. Thank you, Carol. You have been terrific!

From the bottom of our hearts, we express our deep appreciation for the many named and nameless who have contributed to our learning, our growth, our success, our joy and this book, which was born from it all.

CONTENTS

FOREWORD

Stop for a minute and take a look around. Think about the last ten years and imagine the next five. It's easy to see that great change is in the air. One would have to be in an advanced state of denial not to recognize that the world we grew up in is going, going, gone. Of course, there *are* a lot of people in denial. Unfortunately, they tend to be the heads of major organizations and many of our politicians, people whose investment in the status quo blinds them to the new and pressing realities of change.

Most of us, however, are fully, sometimes painfully aware that we are in the midst of what futurist Alvin Toffler calls "the rattling and shaking." We are seeing the fundamental transformation of our lives at work and at home, with no letup in sight, no end to the cultural and economic earthquakes.

Even Peter Drucker, conservative dean of American management theorists, wrote in a recent *Harvard Business Journal* article, "Every few hundred years throughout Western history, a sharp transformation has occurred. In a matter of decades, society altogether rearranges itself—its worldview, its basic values, its social and political structure, its arts, its key institutions. Fifty years later a new world exists. And the people born into that world cannot even imagine the world in which their own grandparents were born. Our age is in such a period of transformation. If history is any guide, this transformation will not be completed until 2010 or 2020."

The forces driving the transformation are many and varied. One is technology, including the unprecedented instant flow of and access to information. Technology is tearing down the traditional boundaries between nations, economies, individuals, the boundaries dividing the haves from the have-nots. The transformation of information technology is making a joke of the regulatory environment that attempts to separate the phone companies from the computer companies from the information technology companies. Information about anything in any form is at the tips of your fingers right in your own home. The result is a "rattling and shaking" of the very infrastructure of work and our personal lives.

Probably a larger driver of the transformation is the absolutely new worldwide marketplace of ideas, capital, manufacturing, and consumers. It is a small and shrinking world with no boundaries. Overnight, the "global economy" is changing the basic free-market formula that was drummed into our belief systems.

My friend and collaborator, Lou Pritchett, former Vice-President of Worldwide Sales for Proctor and Gamble, wrote, "We have yet to see the full impact of the open, global marketplace. By 1997 all raw materials and technology will be available everywhere in the world. *The only differences between countries and markets will be skill levels, education and the level of empowerment of the workforce.*"

Forget about Japan and Germany. They are only part of our present and our children's economic future. Behind them lies the rest of the world. All those countries that we have pejoratively called "third-world" nations or "second-rate" economic powers are just beginning to flex their economic muscles. They want a piece of the pie. They will work hard to get it, and they will play by different rules.

Lester Thurow, the MIT economist, uses the metaphor of games to explain the world economic reality. We play football, a slow, linear game played in a predictable sequence of actions, with lots of time-outs and continual replacement of players.

The rest of the world plays soccer: a fast game in which many things happen at once, a game with very few time-outs and very few replacements.

The rest of the world no doubt regards our game of football much as we regard cricket, the game of the nineteenth century's dominant power, England. We see this slow, archaic, boring, "gentlemanly" game as a relic of another age. And we know it would be easy to compete against.

Looking at us, the rest of the world observes how we have constructed our economy and how we run our companies and thinks we are very easy to compete against And they're right, at least for the moment.

This brings us to the core questions: Given the transformation, given the crushingly competitive world market, how are we, as companies and as a country, going to compete? How can our organizations continually provide world-class solutions at world-class prices? How are we going to develop the new markets, the unthought-of products and services that will keep our standard of living and employment rate high and allow our country to remain a world-class economic power?

Another piece of the puzzle: The people we used to turn to for the answers to such questions, those individuals way up in the corporate tower, no longer have the answers. The world has become too fast and too complex. There is too much information coming from every direction, too many critical variables for one person or a select few to understand the game, much less predict its future. CEOs, directors, and managers—at least those who don't have their heads in the sand—are kept up all night by those questions, but they don't have the answers. Just as distressing, if they have answers, they often cannot implement them fast enough to make a difference.

What fascinates me, as I sit in on meeting after meeting with CEOs and their people, is something I have heard innumerable times, in every kind of industry: the admission by the high-level folks that they do not have the answers. And they're right, they don't. By themselves, they do not know how to increase competitive advantage, how to create innovation, or how to become world-class.

So who has the answers? Who is going to create the solutions large and small, the innovative breakthroughs and the incremental changes that are required for companies to compete in this new game? Where are we to look if (in the words of my friend Mike Szymanczyk of Philip Morris) the formerly omnipotent "corporate gods" are dead?

It is here that the story turns. A new reality is blooming; it is transforming organizations and work.

Every day, all over the business landscape, another company wakes up and realizes that its most underutilized resources are the minds and hearts of its people. It is people—those closest to the customer and closest to the work—who have the answers, who own the solutions.

So what do these well-meaning companies do? They put up suggestion boxes and ask their employees for ideas.

The response, typically, is a deafening silence.

To understand why, you have to understand how we are organized to work. In the nineteenth century, the most efficient and effective organization, the one that stood head and shoulders above the rest, was the army. There you had an autocratic general who saw the "big picture" and passed his orders through captains and lieutenants down to the privates who did the actual grunt work of the organization.

This was the military model, and as the best (i.e., most effective and efficient) large organization model around, it was adopted by rapidly growing companies that were leveraging the industrial revolution and cheap labor. Because it was so successful, the military model influenced the thinking and behavior of generations of managers and CEOs. Universal education in the United States was shaped to support this model. There was a strong autocratic teacher who always had the answers. Promptness was required, silence mandatory. You did your own work. You got a grade. All of these conditions were exactly what was required in factories and offices of the nineteenth and twentieth centuries. Companies wanted "hired hands" who were not paid to think, who checked their brains at the factory gate.

People were managed by fear and coercion. They were given orders and they were given a grade. The company controlled their lives. It was only two or three work generations ago that companies told employees when to get married and where to live.

Why would anybody want to work in that environment? Well, for one thing, workers expected it. The companies had all the power, because they owned the means of production. Second, the governance contract with the "corporate gods" was this: On the job I will do what you say, think what you want me to think, not contradict or go against company codes; in return, you will guarantee me a lifetime of work.

Of course, most of this is no longer true. The contract was broken long ago. People move from job to job in pursuit of more money, better life-styles and schools, greater opportunities. Across the landscape, companies are slashing their work forces to increase productivity and take advantage of technology solutions. As Peter Drucker writes, even control of the means of production, previously owned by the companies in the form of factories, mines, and the like, has shifted. In this age of the information worker, employees truly own a healthy chunk of the means of production.

But with all these changes, we have yet to toss aside the last vestiges of the old military work model. When a company goes to its employees—who have grown up in this system, who only know the military model—and asks them to start thinking, to come up with creative ideas, a lot of questions arise in the minds of those employees.

"Do they mean it?" "Will I lose my job if I contradict my boss?" "What if I tell them what I really think?" and, most painful, "What difference will it make, anyway?"

Underlying these questions are two unnatural and constraining feelings: fear and apathy. By unnatural, I mean they are not part of the normal human makeup. They had to be learned, and our schools and the "military model" workplace have done a good job teaching workers fear and apathy.

W. Edwards Deming, one of the undisputed fathers of the world-wide quality movement, understood this when he wrote that it was the obligation of management to drive fear from the workplace. He would be batting 1.000 if he had added the mandate to drive apathy out of the workplace.

But how do you drive fear out, how do you instill enthusiasm and curiosity in everyone? There are not a lot of guideposts out there; there are no magic bullets, no memos, no simple training programs for accomplishing this.

I believe this is where empowerment and quality efforts get stuck, trying to address the soft, mushy, swampy stuff like fear and apathy. For managers accustomed to working with numbers and hard facts, this "soft stuff" is unnerving and difficult to deal with. Yet, as Tom Malone of the award-winning Milliken Company told an audience recently, "It's the soft stuff that is the hard stuff, but it's the soft stuff that makes the difference."

What is required is nothing less than a re-inventing of the workplace. We must change the structures, the compensation system, the pecking order, the hierarchies so as to better fit the needs of workers who must utilize all their brain power, creativity, and courage in order to tackle the problems of surviving and thriving into the next century. As I see it, we are on the cusp of throwing out all our old notions of how to organize people and tasks around work. We are on the cusp of transforming the workplace.

That is why this is an important book, because pivotal to this transformation is a new kind of leader. It is not the autocratic, "I've got the answers, do what I say" leader. Nor is it the "management by numbers" and the "management by objectives" people. The whole idea of leadership has turned upside down. Today's leaders are there to serve, rather than to be served. They are there to empower people; they don't come to work having the answers. The objective of today's leaders is to help people bring 100 percent of their creativity and courage to bear on the problems of the organization.

In our work at Pecos River Learning Centers in Santa Fe, New Mexico, we say that good leaders do three things. They provide *permission* for their people to try new things, to "get outside of the box." Second, they provide *protection*. Leaders protect their people and their ideas from the corporate immune systems whose job it is to "kill" anything that is new, different, or—God forbid—viewed as a mistake. Finally, leaders provide their people with *processes* to help them tackle and solve problems. When individuals have permission, protection, and processes they flourish, they create, and they can solve problems formerly believed to be insurmountable. At Pecos River Learning Centers we've witnessed this; we've seen the results, and they are nothing short of world-class.

In this thought-provoking and timely book you'll find a virtual tool kit for such leaders. From logical, step-by-step processes for empowerment to tools that will help create a vision of what is possible for a team or group—it's all here. This book should be read and read again. The tools, processes, and questions it provides should become part of the natural work vocabulary of managers and leaders.

So enjoy the book, and remember: if you use it and practice what it teaches, you will be part of the minority of managers and leaders who are taking us into the future of work and a more competitive America.

—LARRY WILSON
*Pecos River Learning Centers,
Santa Fe, New Mexico*

1

GETTING RIGHT TO THE POINT

The significant problems we face today cannot be solved at the same level of thinking we were at when we created them.

ALBERT EINSTEIN

The Challenge to Classical Change Efforts

If someone asked for your advice on a large investment they were considering and told you that the chances of it being successful were only 12% to 15%, what would you advise? How quickly would you want to put some of your own money into this "hot" opportunity? Probably not too quickly.

Yet, every day, business leaders—who should know a bad investment when they see one—invest time, money, and manpower in opportunities offering just such a probability for failure. They invest in change, improvement, and training programs within their organizations, and, while their intentions are good, their returns are not.

A 1988 survey of 3,300 senior managers and human resource professionals made this point clear. The survey, reported by Rob Lebow in his *Washington CEO* magazine article "Making Heroes of Workers," concluded that of the nearly *$48 billion* spent on training and change programs that year *only 12% to 15%* was considered to be money well spent. In other words, 85% to 88% of the time, traditional training and typical approaches to change left business leaders disappointed with the results. This suggests that as much as *$40 billion* was wasted on training and change programs that year.

A leader of a major federal agency reported that his organization spent more than $500,000 over two years on a quality-improvement program. After conducting a survey of their nationwide offices, the management team concluded that the program had been "virtually ineffective." A Fortune 500 corporation spent four years and a tremendous amount of time, energy, and money developing an "architecture for leadership" to improve management abilities within the organization. After they had implemented their new program throughout the company, the feedback they got from a number of their executives and managers suggested that the results were less than expected.

While we do not intend to belittle their efforts, it is important to note that many leaders from varying-sized corporations relate "war stories" of disappointing efforts at change. When talking with board members, stockholders, presidents, managers, and front-line employees throughout North America, we continually hear about their growing frustration with and disappointment in the minimal and short-term results achieved by even the latest and greatest change or improvement efforts. These tensions are tied directly to the colossal sums of money and time spent on programs ranging from motivation to quality control, from customer service to team building, and from cost cutting to strategic planning.

Surely, some people do come out of leadership, quality, or other training programs charged up and ready to apply what they have learned; yet, the majority of these same men and women soon go right back to their old ways of doing things. Few of these programs offer what it takes to make real change occur and have lasting effects within an organization.

One has to wonder why, with so many different consultants, management techniques, and change models, so few programs have good, long-lasting results. Our continuing research indicates that a primary answer to this question lies in the fact that many of these programs *tell* organizations and leaders what they need to do differently, basing this advice on their studies of other organizations' experiences.

This traditional approach to change and improvement does have a certain appeal. It seems easier when someone just gives us the answers. The problems come later when resistance develops, and someone else's approach doesn't work for us.

The traditional methodology used for implementing change or improvement often takes the following steps:

Step 1 Identify the problem.

Step 2 Bring in an expert who seems to understand the problem best, or read in a book
about the latest and greatest "new" solution to the problem.

Step 3 Tell people how to do their jobs differently
and better from the way they have been
doing them.

Step 4 Spend tremendous amounts of time, energy, and money trying to:

(a) overcome the resistance caused by
Step 3, and
(b) make someone else's solution work
for us.

It's not surprising that it takes most companies using
such a process three to five years to implement a quality
program. Most of their time is spent on Step 4—convincing
resistant employees to try something new, making sure they
actually follow through, and force-fitting someone else's
solution to their needs.

Human nature keeps this approach from working effectively. At one time or another, each of us has watched others
doing something and seen a different or better way to accomplish the task. Yet, no matter how much effort we make
in telling them about our way and convincing them to try
it, usually they continue doing it their way. In most cases,
even when we have a common desire for results, they demonstrate resistance to our idea by refusing even to try it.
Or, if others do attempt our way, as soon as we turn our
back they go right back to their same old way of doing it.

We seem intuitively to *know* that the best manner in
which to learn new approaches is to come to the conclusions
ourselves, yet we still want to tell or show people how to do
things a better way. And when the shoe is on the other foot,

we don't want to be told how to do something any more than the next person. The exception to this rule may be in situations where we feel that our way just won't work. Then we may give up and look for guidance, finding comfort in asking someone we deem an expert to come in and give us his or her advice. We may not, however, use their methodology for long. Since it was not our own idea, we may experience resistance or lack commitment to making it work.

A NEW WAY OF MANAGING CHANGE

A recent trade magazine featured a glowing article about a division of a major textile company in North Carolina. The firm had spent hundreds of thousands of dollars with a highly respected, internationally known consulting group to meticulously revamp the company's quality program. The article applauded the consulting company's effectiveness and praised the division's forward-thinking leaders. It also mentioned that after *only* 18 months of changing most of the factory-wide systems, the consultants and management were beginning to conduct sessions with employee groups to generate *enthusiasm* and *commitment* for the new programs. The consultants and executives expressed hope that by using slogans, banners, and meetings to motivate the people, they would begin to see results from the new program *within another year*.

The article stated: "The company is close to being able to celebrate the successful implementation of their new quality program." If one reads between the lines of this article, however, it appears to suggest that they implemented the new systems, encountered their people's initial resistance to change and were now trying to overcome that resistance. Successful implementation was still far from being achieved.

Successes achieved by high-performance organizations

suggest that before there can be any major breakthroughs in motivation, quality, customer service, cost-reduction, or productivity improvement, organizations must deal with the whole issue of change differently. While we support any attempt to help American firms regain leadership in the world market, we see constantly that it does not have to take three to five years—or even 18 months—to realize substantive, enduring results from change programs.

Classical change programs, like the one described in the previous example, seek to implement the systems first and deal with the attitudinal/people problems—like resistance and lack of commitment—later. Trying to overcome resistance late in a change process is like the antiquated and expensive method of fixing a bad product at the *end* of the manufacturing process. We propose that the way to create real and lasting change in this chaotic era is to deal with the issue of attitude/mindset first, or at least concurrently with the system changes. By unleashing and focusing the energy of our people first, we prepare them to support, rather than resist, the changes. Only when a critical mass of its people has taken ownership and responsibility for the needed changes can an organization assure a competitive advantage in today's challenging marketplace. In addition, no one knows what changes are needed better than your own people. The issue is accessing their knowledge and solutions.

Dealing with mindset before implementing change has helped revitalize scores of companies and organizations with which we have worked. Using this method, one New England manufacturing firm went from five consecutive years of losses to a profitable quarter. Moreover, they reaped these benefits the *first* quarter after being introduced to this approach, and the upturn has continued. A New York–based company with an ugly history of union unrest turned months of negative profit-and-loss statements into record-setting productivity within 60 days. They ended the year with the highest profits in their 28-year history and continue to set records in both productivity and profits. Concurrently, management-labor relationships rose to an all-time high.

This book is about the processes used by these and numerous other clients who have helped us fine-tune an effective approach to implementing change on an ongoing basis. It is also about the leadership required for lasting change and how to develop such leadership.

ENLIGHTENED LEADERSHIP

There has been much talk in the business community about the need for visionary leadership, which often is defined as "a leader with a vision of the future." However, many leaders have expressed to us their discomfort with the implied limitations of that terminology, because merely having the vision is not enough to bring about successful organizational change.

What is needed is *enlightened* leadership—leaders who not only have the vision but who have the ability to get the members of the organization to accept ownership for that vision as their own, thus developing the commitment to carry it through to completion.

Taking this concept a step further, Enlightened Leaders actually don't need to have the vision themselves; they need only possess the willingness and ability to draw the vision from their people and inspire and empower those people to do what it takes to bring the vision into reality. Indeed, Enlightened Leaders nurture and encourage their people to be open, creative, and innovative and find what it takes to achieve their shared objectives. They bring out the best in people.

Enlightened Leadership is not so much about things *to do* as it is a place leaders *come from* with whatever they do. It actually is a state of *being*.

How does a leader achieve this seemingly elusive state?

This is just one of the questions we will explore together as we describe a new, unconventional approach to change management. This approach deals directly with people and their attitudes. It reaches into the hearts of organizations and their people. It helps unlock creativity and ingenuity and promotes high-performance teamwork. Daniel Yankelovich, a leading pollster on personal values, talks about "discretionary effort," the amount of energy workers choose to put into their jobs. This approach unleashes people's discretionary efforts and energy so they can be used for the betterment of the organization and for concurrent fulfillment of the individual, thus providing the fuel upon which the organization runs.

The methodologies described will help you focus and align the energy of your people into wholehearted commitment and involvement as your entire team moves together toward implementing change. The approach will show you how to create a cohesive team empowered to effectively face the turbulent challenges of the '90s. Armed with new tools and the personal power to use them, your teams will see problems as opportunities upon which they can build. Every change will become a welcomed, vital part of growth for both the individual and the organization. The tools described can make a significant difference between you and your competition by taking your leadership ability to a new, enlightened level and by empowering your people to create a continuously renewing organization.

There are specific things your organization can do right now to find solutions to current problems and to improve in areas that would better assure a prosperous future, but no one—including us—can give you the answers to your organizational problems. The only answers that will count in the long run are the ones you and your team discover for yourselves, not those someone else discovers for you. On a more positive note, there are an abundance of answers and solutions for virtually every situation or issue your organization currently faces, and they are readily accessible within your organization. In addition, there are no better experts at finding these answers than the people who already work for you.

HOW TO GET THE MOST OUT OF THIS BOOK

In remembering who the *real* experts are, we'd like to talk about what this book can do for you and your organization. Rather than trying to provide a cookie-cutter solution for resolving specific organizational issues, this book provides a foundation for accessing the answers currently present in your organization. Rather than providing you with answers, or telling you what to do, it provides you with questions that present the opportunity for you and your management team to discover *your own* answers. We will guide you in discovering for yourself ways to enhance your leadership ability so that you may tap the spirit of your people and empower them to provide their own solutions to current and future issues.

The successes our clients currently enjoy continue to validate our belief that the only solutions that really work are those they discover for themselves. In the same way, the answers you discover are the ones that *will* work. Your own answers have worked already in the past at those times when your organization has performed particularly well.

If this book is not going to provide you with the answers to the critical issues you and your organization face, what *can* it do? It can:

- **Clarify why traditional efforts at change don't work.**

- **Provide understanding about what the real issues are in dealing with resistance to change.**

- **Introduce an alternative approach that *is* effec-**

tive in generating a change-friendly® climate throughout your organization.

- Present a framework for generating a continuous improvement mindset, which is the key to ongoing organizational renewal.

- Introduce a key leadership tool for getting to the answers/solutions that will work for your team.

- Stimulate solutions for your own unique circumstances.

Will this book deliver on these expectations? We carefully chose our terminology when stating what it *can* do. Its value can be found by applying the age-old concept that we get out of something what we put into it. Whether or not this helps you find the answers to the critical issues and problems facing your organization today depends entirely upon how you apply yourself to the opportunity. Indeed, in its truest form this may be a *work*book.

Coupled with the questions we ask, the information in here helps guide you and your team in systematizing what already works and what could work even better in your organization. To accomplish this goal, however, you must do your part and get involved in the process.

We encourage you to read the questions carefully and to put as much energy into answering them as if they were a test. Your answers are, in fact, being graded, because the results of each and every leader's action in these challenging times are scrutinized by the people who report to them, the people to whom they report, their stockholders, their customers, and their peers. The grade is determined by how well each leader handles the challenges of the '90s and beyond. For this reason, we encourage you to look at these questions as if your future depended upon the answers. *It might*.

Change-Friendly Highlights

1. Many traditional change programs take years to implement.

2. Change can be implemented more quickly and effectively when people's mindsets are dealt with before, or at least concurrently with, system changes.

3. An Enlightened Leader has the ability to get the members of an organization to accept ownership for a vision as their own.

4. This book provides an opportunity to help shape that new model of leadership for your own unique situation.

And in all of my experience, I have never seen lasting solutions to problems, lasting happiness and success, that came from the outside in.

STEPHEN COVEY
The Seven Habits of Highly Effective People

2

THE DYNAMICS OF ORGANIZATIONAL CHANGE

I've been in this business 36 years, I've learned a lot—and most of it doesn't apply anymore.

CHARLES EXLEY
Chairman, NCR Corporation
Wall Street Journal, June 20, 1990

CHANGE OPTIONS

The past decade marked a period of unprecedented change in the world generally and in business markets specifically. Forecasts suggest that the '80s were merely a prelude to the dynamic challenges ahead in the '90s and beyond. Indeed, the entire cycle of change has been altered dramatically. The intervals between changes have shortened and the pace at which change now occurs has quickened. It wasn't long ago that we had time to adjust to change before more change was upon us, but no longer. In today's turbulent marketplace, the only constant is change.

To be successful in today's fast-changing marketplace requires that business be conducted differently than ever before. While yesterday's businesspeople found a degree of comfort and certainty in knowing they could continue doing things "the way we've always done them before," today these words indicate that a manager or a company is already in or headed for trouble. Yesterday we could rely on policies and procedures to assure our people were *doing things right*. Today's highly competitive market demands that our people *do the right things*. Our people must continuously look for new and better ways to accomplish just about everything, sometimes throwing old procedures out the door and leaving that door open for creative and innovative thinking.

The need for innovation is not new, but never before has there been such an urgent demand to *continually* create new and better solutions. For all those working in the business arena, this means that a successful future depends upon the ability to change at least as quickly as the marketplace. Change is a factor that every organization must accept, so how effectively change is implemented becomes more and more critical to the long-term success of an organization.

To clarify some of the issues regarding organizational change, let us look at the typical phases of business development. Larry Wilson, in *Changing the Game: The New Way to Sell,* as well as Dudley Lynch and Paul Kordis in *Strategy of the Dolphin,* have provided excellent treatments of this subject, from which we developed the following.

PHASES OF BUSINESS DEVELOPMENT

Basically, every organization—from one-person start-ups to multibillion-dollar conglomerates—is at some phase of a business growth or development cycle. Some companies remain at one particular phase longer than others. Some do not survive. Some jump from one development cycle to another. However, successful businesses generally go through the same three basic development or growth phases: Entrepreneurial, Growth, and Decline or Renewal.

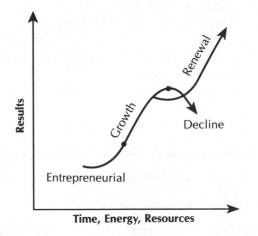

THE FIRST PHASE: ENTREPRENEURIAL

This first interval represents the time of infancy, invention, nurturing, formation, and innovation—entrepreneurship. During this phase, most new businesses scramble to find a successful pattern, develop a better product, deliver exceptional service, and uncover the most effective marketing strategy. Being highly vulnerable, they do whatever it takes to survive and to secure a niche in the market.

The Entrepreneurial Phase usually is filled with excitement and energy. Employees and owners alike are caught up in doing whatever needs to be done, in staying close to the customer and in focusing on how to best serve each person with whom they come into contact. Often marked by discovery and breakthroughs, this phase characteristically involves limited capital and "seat-of-the-pants" existence. High energy and enthusiasm make up for lack of experience and inevitable mistakes.

If one overriding motivation exists among entrepreneurs and their companies, it is a business "itch" that must be scratched, a refusal to give in to the "conventional wisdom" of the established majority.

The Entrepreneurial Phase is marked by:

- **Doing whatever it takes to survive**

- **Adaptability and flexibility to market needs**

- **Willingness to take risks**

- **High motivation and energy**

- **High level of internal and external communication**

Approximately one out of every 10 companies actually outlasts the Entrepreneurial Phase. One day the successful firm will break the code that opens the door to what works, thus moving it into a second development stage. Maybe it finally discovers how to market its product, or learns how to manufacture it efficiently or sees how to deliver its services in a way that differentiates it from the competition. Regardless of how it finds its niche, it launches into a new stage—a period of growth.

THE SECOND PHASE: GROWTH

For the survivors of the first phase, the second stage of development begins with marked growth and expansion. Companies move from the Entrepreneurial Phase into the Growth Phase by having done many things right. In the Growth Phase they begin systematizing their methods so their successes can be replicated effectively. Companies typically keep putting more systems, policies, procedures, and processes into place to sustain and control growth in an attempt to hold on to what they have done that has worked. These structures are important to assure consistency as they grow. They are appropriate early in the Growth Phase.

Early Growth Phase charactcristics include:

- **Market and financial success**
- **Focus on efficiency and effectiveness**
- **Development of systems, rules, and procedures**
- **Shift from entrepreneurial direction to more management control**
- **Excitement about growth**

Later in the Growth Phase, however, those very systems and procedures that have gotten a company successfully to where it is can become barriers to its continued success. Duplication, rigid policies, and assembly-line thinking—all of which we refer to as "boxes"—are indicators of a business late in the second phase of development.

A box is defined by the boundaries of structures, systems, policies, and processes used. A box is usually revealed when someone says, "How about trying it this way?" and is answered, "Oh no . . . we always do it this way around here." It is an area within which an organization operates but does not go beyond.

As the boxes grow stronger, the company becomes less flexible and more rigid, since limitations control any movement outside the box. Any part of the corporate system can become a box impeding creativity. Even formal and informal reward systems and market patterns can and have trapped once-thriving organizations.

The problem is: An organization may have found great solutions in the entrepreneurial phase, but if it becomes too attached to those solutions, yesterday's remedies will likely become tomorrow's problems. Like a barrel approaching Niagara Falls, the box may seem to be a safe haven in the tumultuous rapids. As the market roars ahead, however, the barrel-riders are headed for an inevitable plunge into the turbulence below.

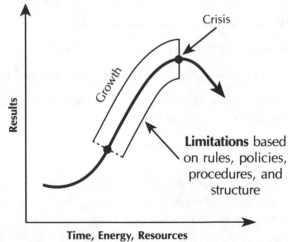

Late in the Growth Phase, the tendency of "boxed companies" is to work harder and harder to do more of what they have been doing all along, and to focus on incremental improvement to the existing systems, procedures, and processes.

When in your career have you felt boxed in or limited in how you could do your job?

What structures or attitudes kept you feeling that way?

When in your career have you felt the greatest freedom to do your job?

What were the factors or circumstances that allowed this freedom?

Growing companies appear to be riding the crest in a steady market-driven upturn, but somewhere ahead a downturn is likely. Even the most successful idea today may prove to be a company's downfall tomorrow. This is a historic fact, and ignoring it only increases the danger.

In *Thriving on Chaos*, Tom Peters writes: "No company is safe. IBM is declared dead in 1979, the best of the best in 1982, and dead again in 1986. People Express is the model 'new look' firm, then flops 24 months later.

"In . . . the foreseeable future, there is no such thing a 'solid,' or even substantial, lead over one's competitors. Too much is changing for anyone to be complacent. Moreover, the 'champ is chump' cycles are growing ever shorter. . . ."

Late Growth Phase characteristics include:

- **Increased number of boxes**
- **Many committees**

- **Breakdown of communications**
- **Habit orientation**
- **Rejection of innovation**
- **Bureaucratic style**
- **Threatened by risk**
- **Low energy**

If we had written this book during the postwar, America-can-do-no-wrong, boom years of 1945 through 1974, we would undoubtedly have focused on the first two development phases. When the economy was less turbulent, the second stage was more predictable, secure, and lasting. Then, companies that had survived well into the Growth Phase could flourish indefinitely even when locked in stifling, uncreative boxes.

Those postwar years conditioned us to believe that what we were doing was what worked. We were wrong. When you are the only ones who have what the world wants, anything works. This false confidence has and still is costing us dearly.

THE THIRD PHASE: DECLINE OR RENEWAL

Every growth cycle has a peak. If we remain locked on this curve past the peak, we move into decline. If we hold on to "what we have always done" or "the way we have always done it around here," we will end up in the Declining or Dying Phase. This is simply what happens when the limitations of our boxes keep us locked on a particular growth curve as it heads downhill—the back side of the curve. Every growth curve has a back side just as surely as it has a front side.

Clearly, no company *consciously* chooses to go into a

gradual decline or a sudden tailspin any more than the crew of the *Titanic* chose to ram into an iceberg. Some companies don't even realize they have passed into decline until it is too late to respond to the impending disaster caused by the imperceptible changes. Unfortunately, organizations locked in their boxes are likely to continue "the way we do things here" until a crisis does occur—when growth peaks and starts down the back side of the curve.

When a crisis occurs, it is vital to understand the real nature of the possible choices. One option is to work harder inside the boxes. That's a little like swabbing the deck on the *Titanic*. When the ship was undamaged and thought to be unsinkable, keeping the decks clean was a prudent thing to do. With a gaping hole in its hull, swabbing decks because "it's what we've always done" doesn't make much sense.

While no one consciously chooses to decline, some companies do it unconsciously by staying in their boxes or barrels or making no choice at all, unaware of the dangerous rapids ahead until it is too late. Those unable to break out of the boxes die every day. Their obituaries are published regularly in *The Wall Street Journal, Barron's, Fortune, BusinessWeek,* and other publications.

However, there is another option: to consciously break

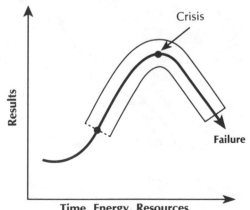

out of the boxes and move into an entirely new growth cycle—the Renewal Phase. The market changes around us continuously, and, as it does so, possibilities for new growth curves/cycles are created. To renew means to begin again, revitalize, give new spiritual strength, make new again, make strong again, bring back into good condition. Renewal requires a conscious choice. It requires a return to the long-lost entrepreneurial spirit. Renewal of an organization requires renewal of its people.

We do not have to wait until a crisis occurs to renew. Through conscious choice and anticipation of the need to change, we can jump off the old growth curve and onto a new one before the old one turns downward and before we run up against the limitations of our structures and processes. This requires that we operate out of a strategic mindset that is attuned to the future.

When asked about the secret of his success, Wayne Gretzky, arguably one of history's greatest professional hockey players, replied, "I skate to where the puck is going to be, not where it has been." A business leader's challenge, currently and in the future, is to "skate to where the puck is going to be." We must anticipate where the market is going and will be, not where it is or has been.

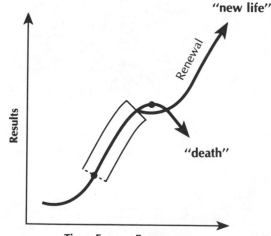

> *What is your organization doing right now to prepare for where the market will be one year from now? Three years from now?*
>
> *What could you be doing differently to better anticipate corporate or marketplace changes?*
>
> *How would your organization be better positioned today if it could have better anticipated the needed changes it now faces?*
>
> *What benefits have you received when you have successfully anticipated corporate or marketplace changes?*

Program
Flexibilty

— less
people

S P Book / Show

A flexible, anticipatory mindset is one of the best foundations upon which to build, for it offers a perspective that allows for possibilities that may not be visible from a crisis- or evolutionary-bounded vista. Top priority for any corporation seeking a strategic advantage today should be to develop a mindset among its people that naturally anticipates and supports ongoing renewal.

The dynamics of our world marketplace today require that we continually be in a process of renewal. However, new systems alone are not the answer. If we simply change from one system to another, the new system soon becomes another box. Instead, we must create a completely new way of thinking—a trail-blazing perspective from which we view the present and the future.

Larry Wilson says: "All organizations seem to go through phases of growth. It's simply the natural way that businesses evolve. What we're seeing today, and what is critical to our strategic understanding, is that most businesses, almost our entire economy, are going through the turbulence of phase change—moving into a third phase, reinventing business."

The Renewal Phase is marked by the following characteristics:

- **Reawakening, revitalization**
- **Closeness to customers and market**
- **Willingness to take risks**
- **Change-friendly mindsets**
- **Quality orientation**
- **Rekindling of the entrepreneurial spirit**
- **Openness and flexibility**

What new idea holds the greatest potential for gain in your area of responsibility?

What will it take to have it work?

If your idea did work, what would be the benefits for your organization and yourself?

PERSONAL GROWTH CYCLE

Creating a renewing organization requires having renewing people within that organization. In fact, the development curve for business, particularly the Growth and Declining/Dying or Renewal Phases, fits the lives of individual people as well. As we learn what we must do to thrive, or get by, or survive in life, we define structures, processes, and procedures for ourselves that we know work. We call them habits. Most of these habits were established very early in our lives from the various ways we were "programmed" or conditioned by those who most influenced us.

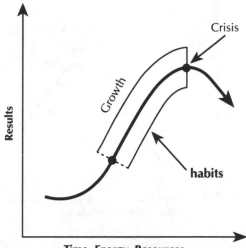

Just as businesses form boxes with policies, procedures, and processes, the habits we form create boxes that determine boundaries for the way we do things. As long as we are locked into "the way we've always done things," outcomes are predictable, so our lives seem somewhat comfortable and safe. Those feelings of safety are somewhat misleading, however, as every growth curve, including a personal one, has a back side, a downturn, a declining or dying phase. By staying locked in our boxes, we are sure to ride the curve over the peak and down the back side to our "death"—perhaps emotional death.

The issue here is that the habits we formed years ago, which were perfectly valid for what we needed at the time, are not necessarily valid now. We may have learned from a parent or someone else close to us to "do it this way (because I told you to)." While "this way" may have been well founded in that specific situation, it may be totally ineffective for the situation in which we now find ourselves. Yet, we continue to do it "this way," because it is the way we learned. Our mindset, or paradigm, is "that's the way it *should* be done."

Just as with organizations, if we are locked in our per-

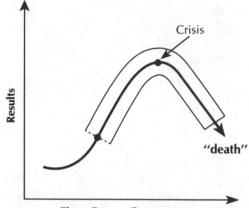

Time, Energy, Resources

sonal boxes we will eventually run simultaneously into the limitations of the box and into a downturn in our growth curve. This point represents crisis. Crisis in our individual lives is sometimes scary. It may look like serious physical or mental illness, divorce, loss of a loved one, loss of a job, or loss of a promotion. The fall down the back side of the curve after a crisis can be rapid, and for many people it can be difficult to recover and begin a new curve. Some never do. However, the positive side is that crisis usually stimulates us to stop and look at our boxes, the paradigms from which we are living.

Change is constant for individuals, just as it is for organizations. If we choose to hold our own, stay in our boxes, and not continually grow, we will eventually find ourselves in crisis. Every growth curve does peak and turn downward. Our choice is to hang on to "the way we always do things" and ride down the dying side or break out of our boxes and jump onto a brand-new upward curve of renewal. It is important to note that we do not have to suffer an awakening personal crisis to renew. We can choose to live in a state of continuous renewal at any time.

CONTINUOUS RENEWAL

An important aspect to look at concerning the Renewal Phase is that renewal is not a one-time event. In the dynamics of our current marketplace, renewal must be an ongoing, never-ending process. It is not a destination but a journey. Like the Enlightened Leader, renewal is not something to *do*—it is a mindset or culture, a place effective organizations and people *come from*.

The process of continuous renewal—that process of the ongoing quest for how to do it more and more effectively—requires a particular mindset that is usually found naturally in top performers. Recognizing the importance and need for change is the mark of a healthy, renewing person or organization. This ability to be flexible and highly adaptable requires an attitude of openness and opportunity, rather than a mindset dominated by problems and fear. We call this renewing attitude change-friendly. People must make a conscious effort to become change-friendly, because becoming a change-friendly person in a change-friendly organizational environment is essential for *creating* the future instead of waiting for it to arrive.

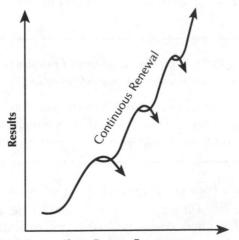

Inspired by computer lingo, the term change-friendly comes from "user-friendly," which means easy-to-work-with, responsive, adaptive, compatible, problem resistant, and forgiving of mistakes. In addition, when computers were a new commodity, user-friendly meant that even those who had never used a computer would find the adjustment an easy one with a user-friendly system. In short, user-friendly software or equipment enables people to do their jobs with maximum facility and effectiveness and with minimal interference and restriction.

Thus, to be change-friendly, an organization must be able to anticipate, understand, deal effectively with, and even benefit from the change process. A change-friendly organization enables and empowers its people to do their jobs with maximum facility and effectiveness and with minimal interference and restriction. Above all else, a change-friendly organization is open to new ideas and approaches, free of the fear of taking risks.

A change-friendly person possesses the same qualities as a change-friendly organization. In fact, one who truly understands this concept will be invigorated by the possibilities that would rarely come without accelerated change. The very best performers tend to be change-friendly.

> *What would be the long-term benefits if your people were more change-friendly?*
>
> *In what ways would it benefit you and your organization if you had a straightforward way to create a change-friendly environment?*

Adds Tom Peters: "If the word 'excellence' is to be applicable in the future, it requires wholesale redefinition. Perhaps : 'Excellent firms don't believe in excellence—only in constant improvement and constant change.' That is,

excellent firms of tomorrow will cherish impermanence—
and thrive on chaos."

Continuously renewing organizations stay on the leading
edge of the change curve. They anticipate change. They
adapt quickly and effectively to needed changes. To survive
and thrive in the '90s and beyond requires that organizations become change-friendly and continuously renewing.

The people in a renewing organization have a continuous
improvement/continuous renewal mindset. In other words,
they constantly look for better ways of doing everything
they do from the quality of their interactions and communications to the effectiveness of procedures they use. It
is the development of this mindset of continuous renewal/
improvement that is our challenge as leaders.

Renewing organizations require Enlightened Leaders
who can bring out the best in their people—their people's
innovation, their ability to anticipate the future, their ability
to make it work. In so doing, these leaders inspire a consciousness of continuous renewal in their people.

Change-Friendly Highlights

1. During the past decade, American business may have experienced the most turbulent time in history.

2. If present trends continue, organizational environments will be more unpredictable than ever during the coming decade—perhaps more so than most analysts are forecasting.

3. The myriad obstacles facing organizations today demand fundamentally new modes of thinking and responding.

4. Only the most flexible, creative, adaptable systems will be able to convert today's challenges into exciting and rewarding opportunities for their organizations and their people.

5. A leader's challenge is to renew continuously, to anticipate change—to anticipate where the market will be, not where it is or has been.

6. The ability to be flexible, highly adaptable, and anticipatory requires a particular mindset, an attitude of openness and opportunity.

Our options are to learn this new game, the rules, the roles of the participants and how the rewards are distributed, or to continue practicing our present skills and become the best players in a game that is no longer being played.

LARRY WILSON
Changing the Game: The New Way to Sell

3

GETTING TO THE *REAL* ISSUES

We tend to meet any new situation by reorganizing, and a wonderful method it can be for creating the illusion of progress while producing confusion, inefficiency and demoralization.

PETRONIUM
Greek Philosopher (210 B.C.)

SYMPTOMS OF THE PROBLEM

Leaders typically report that the most critical issues they face include quality, service, profitability, cost control, productivity, and/or overall performance. These issues often take the form of poor quality, declining profits, productivity drop-offs, sales downturns, and unacceptable customer service. These organizational difficulties represent some of the *hard issues*.

- whs
- Purchasing
- Delivery
  Sales
  System
- Quality of Staff

> *What are your two or three most pressing organizational issues—issues that, if you could resolve them, would place you in the best position to achieve your objectives?*

In reality, these issues represent only the symptoms of the real, underlying problems. Many organizations tend to deal primarily with these symptoms time and again, rarely digging deeper to find their source. As with symptoms of physical illness, if the doctor merely treats the symptoms and doesn't treat the cause of the problem, the symptoms will persist or return.

Many leaders tend to focus on hard issues because they are easy to see, recognize, and measure, and in some ways, they seem to be easier to address. Leaders also place importance on hard issues because they seemingly are based on fact, and factual matters can be debated, proven, and strategized. In addition, for most of us, it is more comfortable to address these concrete, nonhuman issues.

Yet, addressing hard issues just because they are more tangible and measurable is being like the proverbial drunk who looks futilely for his keys half a block away from where he lost them, reasoning that "there is no street light down there." Focusing on the hard issues because the means to

address them seem clear does not make the problems—
only the symptoms—go away. Real problems do not often
go away when ignored.

THE REAL ISSUE

The underlying cause of hard issues is often found in
the *soft issues* of an organization. *The soft issues are the
human issues*—the fundamental attitudinal or mindset issues of our people. These soft issues consist of less tangible
aspects that are much more subjective and less easily measured or charted than the hard issues. In addition, we are
probably less experienced in dealing with these people
issues.

For our purposes, we use attitude and mindset interchangeably, because their meanings are quite similar. *Web-
ster's New World Dictionary* (Third College Edition)
defines attitude as one's disposition, opinion, mental set.
Mindset is defined as a fixed mental attitude formed by
experience, education, prejudice. State of mind can also be
used accurately for this concept.

Dealing with the true cause of a problem often involves
understanding and fostering attitudinal changes in people.
When we talk about attitude or mindset, we are not just
talking about "positive attitude" or "negative attitude." Positive and negative make up just a small part of our overall
attitude, mindset or state of mind. Our general mental and
emotional well-being, self-image, self-esteem, values, beliefs, and feelings about the world and our place in it all
affect our state of mind.

An individual's performance is directly related to his/her
state of mind—a soft issue. Performance, which can often
be measured, is a hard issue. State of mind is a soft issue.
An effective mindset creates good performance and desirable results.

Recall a time you grudgingly had to do a project at work when you would have preferred to be doing something else. How long did it take you to complete the task?

What was the quality of your work?

How did your attitude affect the outcome of the project?

Much of American management doesn't seem willing or equipped to address directly what is often the real issue—their people's mindset. Referring to such issues as "touchy-feely" or "none of our business," they hope that sooner or later the system or structure changes themselves will gain enough support from their people to be successful. Plus, they tend to think of hard issues as more important than soft issues. They tend to deal with soft issues poorly and only as a last resort, often when it is too late to make a difference.

A top executive of a well-known corporation provided a good example of this "wishful thinking" mentality when during our first conference he skipped the small talk and went straight to the bottom line: "We have two divisions in our company that are doing poorly, so we have brought in two groups of consultants and spent a lot of money to design programs to bring about major changes. One program has been going for 14 months, and the other has been going for two years. My managers tell me they will need three to five years to get each program operational and fully accepted. Yet, to be brutally honest, I haven't seen any results yet.

"I just don't see how we can accept poor workmanship and negative attitudes any longer and survive. Doesn't it make sense that if we get the systems, structures and processes working right, then our people will take care of themselves?"

What *"hard" issues have you poured resources into with less than satisfactory results?* credits/whs

---

This belief that our soft issues will disappear if we get our systems, structures, and processes right has caused the downfall of many organizational change efforts. Soft issues do not just go away. It's the pay now or pay later plan. Just like waiting to fix an assembly at the very end of the manufacturing line, the longer we wait to resolve the issue, the more we have invested in the problem and the more expensive it is to deal with. We have to deal with problems head-on at some point.

According to John F. Welch, Jr., chairman and CEO of General Electric Company, "We've spent the majority of our energy in the '80s working, appropriately, on the *hardware* of American business because that hardware had to be fixed. But hardware has limits. The Japanese, on the other hand, have the software, the culture which *ties productivity to the human spirit*—which has practically no limits.

"That's where we have to turn in the '90s—to the *software* of our companies—to the culture that drives them.

"To change that culture radically, and I believe in most cases radically is the word, we have to move beyond the start we got in the '80s. We have to move from the incremental to the radical, toward a fundamental *revolution in our approach to productivity and to work itself*—a revolution that must touch every single person in the organization every business day.

"How do we get big companies back to their roots—back

to the type of spirit and fire that creates miracles in those garage start-ups in Silicon Valley before they get big and before they forget what *made* them big? That's what we're talking about. Nothing less."

What Welch is referring to is what we call renewal—rekindling of the spirit of an organization's people and refocusing that revitalized energy on what needs to be done. What we must do is deal with the people issues, the soft issues, to accomplish this renewal. Leaders who can directly address these mindset issues of our people are needed—Enlightened Leaders.

What are the soft or people issues that are keeping your organization from achieving the hard objectives important to your surviving and thriving? Limited inititive / skills

As you look at the critical issues in your organization, what's making the most sense about this?

THE IMPORTANCE OF MINDSET TO PERFORMANCE

Organizations cannot hope to overcome or overpower problems simply by instituting new programs, systems, or policies. Certainly system and process changes are important, and if the systems and processes are outdated or are not effective for any reason, even a shift in attitude is not going to have the company function as well as it can.

Conversely, even with the "latest and greatest" systems and processes, an organization's performance is limited severely without the cooperative attitudes and support of its people. By focusing attention on structures, systems, and processes—the tangible side of the change issues—organizational leaders seem to ignore the fact that the company's performance is linked directly to the attitudes of its people.

A major cardboard carton manufacturer in the Pacific Northwest reported a 25% increase in productivity during all three shifts on one major cutting machine three weeks after the supervisor of that department resigned. This supervisor's attitude was that shift workers should do the job because "I told them to," while his successor was a natural Enlightened Leader who took an interest in his people and how they thought things should be done. After thorough analysis of what caused the productivity increase, only one factor emerged—a change in the attitude of the people due to the supervisory change.

In what ways do you recognize that the attitudes of your people affect the results they achieve?

In what ways do you notice that your mindset affects your own performance?

SYSTEMS AND PROCESSES VS. THE HUMAN FACTOR

Many organizations work hard on the systems and processes side and seem to leave out this critical piece—the human factor—until forced to deal with low productivity, major resistance to change, high error levels, increased absenteeism, or numerous other attitudinal symptoms. When resistance to change can no longer be ignored because problems have reached a crisis level, it is all the more difficult to deal with people's mindsets. The stress of crisis presents a difficult environment for dealing with attitudinal issues. Yet, when we are in crisis, the mindset issues of our people are the most critical issues to manage.

Many managers feel that just doing something about the systems and processes will achieve the desired results. They talk about quality systems. They quote from the quality gurus, J. M. Juran, W. Edwards Deming, and Phillip Crosby, yet they still struggle with quality problems. By just focusing on the quality *systems* they fail to address the fundamental issue, which is the attitude people bring with them to the job.

Wrote Lee Iacocca, former chairman of Chrysler Corporation: "Every day in America, 242 million people wake up, and if everyone would say when he gets up that he's going to do some classy, quality thing today that he didn't do yesterday, we'd be world beaters. Unfortunately, most people swing out of bed, yawn, and figure: 'Oh hell, I've got to make it through another day of drudgery.' The attitude is that they're going to do what they're told and not one thing more. Now, how can you ever improve anything that way?"

The former automaker added: "Quality, after all, is affected by something as basic as a person's sense of values. . . . If a person's going to do a good job, he's got to like coming to work. He's got to say to himself: 'I'm going to help produce something great today,' and he's got to say that every day." Iacocca understands the importance of the human factor.

Other soft issues are critical as well. As Dr. Deming, who has been credited with taking the concept of quality awareness to Japan and revitalizing quality in the United States, so often says, "He that starts with statistical methods alone will not be here in three years." Deming adds that what is needed is "a bedrock philosophy of management, with which statistical methods [are] consistent."

It takes only a brief look at his management philosophy to realize Dr. Deming is more insightful about what needs to be done in American industry than he is sometimes credited with being. He clearly sees the criticality of people's attitudes within the total vision. Rather than suggesting more structure, Deming suggests ". . . a transformation of management. Structures have been put in place by management that have to be dismantled. They have not been suitable for two decades. They never were right, but in an expanding market you couldn't lose. The weaknesses showed up when competition came in. We will have to undergo a total demolition of American style of management. . . ."

As a result of seeing Deming only as a statistician supporting the implementation of Statistical Process Control (SPC), many organizations have been frustrated with the level of effectiveness of their quality programs. SPC only measures the *results* of the methods and attitudes about quality that people bring with them to the job. No matter how good we get in measuring the statistics, SPC alone doesn't change those attitudes. In fact, implementing SPC without addressing the mindsets first actually can *cause* a great deal of the resistance to change, a mindset issue.

DEALING WITH MINDSET—FIRST

What happens when an organization—however well intentioned—tries to change the structures and processes first? Invariably there is a degree of resistance, usually substantial. Much energy is then wasted on overcoming this resistance to change. This resistance actually negates much of the value of the process changes that are sometimes vitally needed. Yet, the classical approach to change has us first implement system, structure, or process changes to deal with a problem, then expend tremendous energy and resources trying to overcome resistance to the changes, attempting to gain buy-in for them from the people.

There is an alternative, however, an approach to change

that actually generates buy-in and commitment before, or concurrent with, implementing the change. The approach is to deal with the mindset issues first, or at least concurrently with system and process changes. Our clients' experiences validate that with this approach to implementing change, their people begin approaching change from a different perspective. They begin to approach it with an attitude that includes an openness to change and the ability to see the opportunity in change—a change-friendly attitude. We see this subtle distinction, between causing the resistance and accessing people's natural desire to make a difference and to feel a part of what's going on, as a primary *key* to the renewal of any organization.

Leaders' understanding of this distinction and their ability to act accordingly will clearly distinguish them from those fighting to get into, struggling to hold on to a portion of, or even surviving in the marketplace. Their companies will become the industry leaders.

While changes in systems and processes are essential, leaders cannot hope to achieve success in implementing them without a broad base of support from their people. Refusing to address the core issues—the mindset and spirit of their people—dooms an organization and its people to constant firefighting, conflicts, and high levels of stress.

Yet, dealing with soft issues is a lot easier than many leaders believe, and dealing directly with the soft issues provides the most effective long-term impact on change efforts. In the dynamically changing business environment of today, we can no longer afford to ignore these soft issues and hope they take care of themselves.

Enlightened Leaders know this and continually search for ways to manage the attitudes, thus the energy and commitment, of their people. Indeed, they deal with these mindset issues consciously and continuously as a requirement for creating a change-friendly, renewing environment. They also do it not in a manipulative way but in a way that benefits all concerned.

Change-Friendly Highlights

1. The majority of American organizations are oriented toward spotting and dealing with only the symptoms of problems instead of their root causes.

2. Symptoms, or "hard" issues—poor quality, productivity drop-offs, declining profits, sales downturns, and unacceptable customer service—are certainly problems, but they are primarily indicators of the real, or "soft" issues—attitudes, mindsets, and states of mind.

3. Soft issues are human issues and seemingly cannot be measured. It is these people issues, however, that directly impact the hard issues and, therefore, the bottom line.

4. Even with the most up-to-date systems and processes, an organization's performance is limited severely without cooperative attitudes and the support of its people. The real issue is the collective attitude of the people in an organization.

5. Many business leaders have seized on W. Edwards Deming's ideas to support their own concepts of changing the processes and systems. However, their misunderstanding of his ideas subsequently has been used to justify their not dealing with attitudinal issues.

6. Structures and processes are important, and they go hand in hand with attitudes. Our reason for emphasizing the attitudinal side is that many organizations work very hard on the structures and process side and seem to ignore a critical piece: attitude.

Any fact facing us is not as important as our attitude toward it, for that determines our success or failure.

NORMAN VINCENT PEALE

4

THE MINDSET ISSUE

*Lasting improvement does not take place by
pronouncements or official programs.
Change takes place slowly inside each of us
and by the choices we think through in quiet
wakeful moments lying in bed just before
dawn.*

PETER BLOCK
The Empowered Manager

The 80%/20% Differences

Take any new idea—an improved process or an advanced technology—and introduce it to any given group of people. The reaction of these people will usually follow the 80/20 Rule of Thumb, or Pareto's Principle. About 20% of the people will be open to the change, or change-friendly. These are the same 20% that are providing 80% of the effective work. They will naturally operate from a mindset that sees the value of whatever change is introduced, and they will be open to it. The other 80% can usually be counted on to resist the change to some degree, no matter how much sense it makes.

Regardless of what change is implemented, the change-friendly 20%ers tend to readily take it in stride. These people will begin looking for ways to make change work, will add improvements, and will continue doing a good job. Some will even support the change without thoroughly understanding it or knowing why it is necessary. We can usually count on these 20%ers to be "on board" with little coaxing.

However, the remaining 80%ers typically do not accept change so naturally. They may even unconsciously sabotage the new system. This sabotage may show up in subtle ways, such as lowered effort and energy, sloppy work, grumbling, complaining, tardiness, missed days, or lack of commitment. They may even try to prove the new way doesn't work.

Of course, if our organizations could depend entirely on the 20%ers, we would not have to worry much about motivation, overcoming resistance to change or putting effort into increasing productivity and improving quality. In most organizations, though, the dissension of the 80%ers means that the 20%ers have to carry much more than their own weight to make the change effective. Unfortunately, the inclination is for the 80%ers to influence the 20%ers more than vice versa. The 80%ers tend to be the critical mass and sustain a negative chain reaction against virtually any desired change. They're like a wet blanket snuffing out the fire of change before it becomes strong enough to sustain itself.

ATTITUDE

The difference between the 20%ers and the 80%ers comes down to one simple overriding element: *attitude*. This is the same fundamental soft issue discussed in the previous chapter. Attitude relates to all of our mental and feeling perspectives, not just the popular positive-versus-negative judgments. Our perceptions, for instance, are an area dramatically impacted by our overall mindset.

Take rain as an example. To a family camping out during a week's vacation, rain could ruin everything. To the photographer, rain means a simple change on his or her f-stop setting. To the farmer caught in a summer's drought, rain can save not only that year's crop but the family farm as well. To someone else, it may be the perfect excuse to stay home and read a good book. To NASA authorities, it may mean a shuttle re-entry delay. *Actually, it is just rain— our attitudes add all the rest.*

For example, Ms. Beasley, the manager of a service department, schedules a meeting with her team. During the first 10 minutes of that conference, she outlines a procedure change—a new way of handling customer complaints.

Janice, who has been with the company for three years and does an excellent job, hears this new procedure and thinks: "All right. Yeah, I can see how that would work. In fact, it'll save me time every day. I can do my daily reports more easily with the new procedure. I like that Ms. Beasley. She keeps coming up with good ideas."

Sitting next to Janice, Sam listens to Ms. Beasley's comments and his mind races. "Cripes! Why is she doing this to us?" he wonders. "Is this her way of telling us that we haven't been doing it right? The old way has worked just fine for years."

Billie, on the other side of Janice, thinks, "Not another new idea from old lady Beasley. You know, I can see where it might save time, but I just learned the old way of doing things, and I don't want to start all over. I'd rather do it the way I've been doing it."

All three team members have listened to the same words. They have the same supervisor and work within the same system. The only real difference is in the perceptions of Janice, Sam, and Billie. The difference is in their attitudes or mindsets, thus in their responses.

> *How have you been frustrated recently by individuals or a group who resisted an idea of yours, regardless of how good you thought the idea was?*

A summary of the differences between the 20% and 80% mindsets, two extreme ways of thinking, is reflected in the figure on the opposite page. We refer to the 80%ers as Reactive Thinkers and the 20%ers as Creative Thinkers. It is important to note that this is not an either/or situation. Each of us is somewhere on the continuum between these two extremes at any moment. And each of us moves up and down the line to some degree depending on the circumstances surrounding us and our versatility—another mindset issue.

In our eighteen-year study of outstanding performance, scores of teams have validated that attitude as by far the dominant factor separating high performance Creative Thinkers from their less productive Reactive Thinkers counterparts. While none of us have control of all the circumstances in our lives, we do have control over our attitude, thus how we perceive those circumstances. Though we may not always be able to choose the circumstances ourselves, we can choose how we *respond* to them. We have a choice every moment of every day about how we look at circumstances, about what attitude we will have in reference to them. Though it may not always be easy in difficult situations to maintain the most effective attitude, or respond effectively, we *do* have the choice.

Extreme Thinking Styles

B

Creative Thinkers

Are open to change.
Are "can do" oriented.
Build on successes and strengths.
Seek the opportunity in situations .
Take responsibility for their actions.
Think in terms of new possibilities.
Are good listeners.
Have a continuous supply of energy.
Make choices & decisions easily.
Feel in control of their environment.
Get results without trying hard.
Are driven to excel by challenge/risk.
Enjoy an inner calmness.
Are current & future oriented.
Learn & grow from their mistakes.
Have high self-esteem.
Focus on results they want.
Do the right things.

A

Reactive Thinkers

Are resistant to change.
See reasons they *cannot* do things.
Focus on finding problems to fix.
Are blinded by problems in a situation.
Avoid blame or responsibility.
Are limited by what worked in the past.
Are poor listeners.
Run out of energy quickly.
Find it difficult to choose & decide.
Feel they have no control of environment.
Often work very hard.
Are afraid of risks or major challenges.
Suffer excessive inner stress.
Cannot let go of the past.
Are devastated by failure.
Have low self-esteem.
Focus on what they want to avoid.
Do things right.

PERFORMANCE

THINKING STYLE

Notice how performance reflected in this figure relates directly to ways of thinking. In what ways might you relate this to your own people?

Think about two or three of the best people in your organization, the ones upon which you know you can count. What specific factors differentiate these top performers from the rest of your team?

How many of those factors are primarily attitude-based vs. knowledge- or skill-based?

Review the list of characteristics describing Reactive and Creative Thinking. How many of these factors are predominantly attitude-related vs. skill- or knowledge-based?

Reactive Thinkers often play the role of victim. They see the problems they face as circumstantial, so they think they are powerless to do anything about them. They tend to respond quite reactively to problems that occur or changes that are proposed. Creative Thinkers, on the other hand, take responsibility for their attitudes and for their responses to circumstances. Coming from this position, they are likely to respond to problems faced or changes proposed more maturely and effectively.

While the attitude factor plays an important role for each of us as individuals, imagine how critical it is for the teams of individuals we lead. Leaders must be clear about the pivotal role played by the attitude of individual team members and the organization's collective attitude. Once clear about the critical impact of attitude on performance, we must invest the necessary energy to develop an understanding about how we as leaders already impact the attitudes of our people and how we would do so more consciously and effectively. Enlightened Leaders have this awareness and continually expand and refine their ability to manage the attitudes of their people.

After working with us, Larry Ramirez, general manager of Container Corporation of America in Renton, Washington, puts it this way: "A lot of people's minds have been opened to the fact that attitude has by far the biggest impact on success and that the old adage that attitudes can't be changed is a falsehood. Now we realize the tremendous impact that this shift in attitudes has on our success, on the empowerment of our people, and how easy it really is to manage. It's exciting to see what's happening.

In what ways do differences in attitudes show up in your people?

How would you describe the collective attitude of your organization?

What would be the long-term impact on your organization's effectiveness if you could have more of your people operating naturally as Creative Thinkers?

WHAT KEEPS PEOPLE FROM MAINTAINING AN EFFECTIVE ATTITUDE?

One of leadership's key roles is to bring out the best in people. Since attitude is so critical to performance, it is essential for leaders to understand what keeps people from choosing and maintaining an attitude that would best serve them and their organizations. More and more evidence points to self-image, or self-esteem, as the key factor in this issue.

How we perceive ourselves and how we believe others perceive us defines our self-image. In addition, how we perceive ourselves directly impacts our self-esteem—our belief in ourselves, our self-respect, our feelings of self-worth. In turn, much of our behavior is based on what we believe and how we feel about ourselves and our environment. (We consider the concepts of self-image and self-esteem synonymous.)

Our self-image is made up of positive and negative thoughts, beliefs or feelings we have about ourselves, as illustrated below, in Figure 1. They are all perceptions about ourselves.

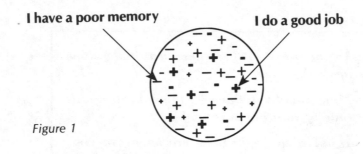

I have a poor memory   **I do a good job**

Figure 1

Figure 2 shows a more positive self-image, people who think more about their strengths, because they have more positive self-image components than negative.

Figure 2

Figure 2 also more accurately models the attitude of the 20%ers/Creative Thinkers. When we perceive ourselves in a more positive light and we feel good about ourselves, we

For additional tips on maintaining an effective attitude, call 1-800-798-9881 and ask for a complimentary copy of "Team Health Indicators."

tend to have a more positive, open-minded outlook in general.

Figure 3 reflects a less positive, or a negative self-image, and represents people who generally think more about what's wrong with themselves. They have more negative self-image components than positive.

Figure 3 more accurately suggests the mindset of the 80%ers/Reactive Thinkers. When we are more heavily focused on what we have become conditioned to think is

Think about a time when you might have had a setback of some kind. How was your attitude affected by the thoughts and feelings you were having?

How were you likely to respond to a difficult situation while in that frame of mind?

How would that frame of mind, or attitude, most likely affect your performance?

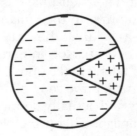

Figure 3

wrong with us, when we don't feel very good about ourselves, we tend to have a more negative, closed-minded
outlook in general.

When we experience setbacks, many of us who are normally more Creative Thinkers tend to slip down the Reactive-Creative scale and operate more from the Reactive
mode. We have all experienced times, however, when we
operated much more effectively from the Creative Thinking
mode, possibly because we had recently been recognized
for what we had done or were doing.

> *Think about another time when you were
> feeling good about yourself, perhaps after a
> recognized success. What was your general
> attitude?*
>
> *In what ways were you better equipped to
> deal with difficult situations in this frame of
> mind?*
>
> *How did this attitude affect your perfor-
> mance?*

Many salespeople can relate to how attitude affects performance. Let's say a salesperson has an annual quota that
he or she is absolutely expected to accomplish. Until that
quota is achieved, many people feel a great deal of pressure
to achieve that goal. Their self-image is at stake. They must
achieve the goal to prove to their manager and peers—as
well as to themselves—that they are an okay person in
general and a good salesperson in particular. The belief in
this scenario is, "If I don't make quota, I am not okay." This
inner focus on trying to prove yourself to be a worthy person
uses a lot of energy and actually detracts from the very job
you want to accomplish. This principle is equally true for
workers in any environment or career.

An amazing thing happens once that salesperson's quota is achieved. Suddenly, selling becomes easier. Many salespeople perform far more effectively after they have achieved their quota. Once they have protected their self-image by achieving quota, their mindset shifts, and they can relax. They can stop trying to prove themselves worthy. They don't come across to customers as needy, but as someone who wants to serve.

The key is the attitude/mindset shift that occurs when they make that magic quota. They have proven (at least temporarily) to the world and, more important, to themselves that they are an okay person and a good salesperson. What results is an inner confidence in themselves—perhaps the most fundamentally important factor in sales or any other kind of success. At least for a period of time, their self-image is more positive.

This "already-made-quota" mindset is the continuous state of mind of true Creative Thinkers and is not dependent upon external circumstances like quota performance. The attitude they show the world reflects this perspective and so does their performance. This self-confidence, or high level of self-esteem, is consistently found in truly outstanding performers regardless of their job or function.

As Stephen Covey discusses in *The Seven Habits of Highly Effective People,* they are response-*able*. They are *able* to choose responses (to external circumstances) that best serve them, rather than automatically react. Notice the difference in attitude in any work environment (e.g.,

---

What would be the value if you could have the majority of your people operating from the magical mindset of having "already made quota" throughout the year?

manufacturing) where performance is "over quota." People feel good about what they are doing, thus they feel good about themselves. Self-confidence is boosted, and even *higher* levels of performance and satisfaction can be achieved.

THE DEVELOPMENT OF SELF-IMAGE

The human mind is much like a computer. While it is far more complex and powerful than any computer devised by man, many, if not all, of its abilities are dependent upon how it is programmed or conditioned. In a general sense, our basic self-image is formed through programming or conditioning that begins at least by the time of birth and extends to the present. Many behavior experts, child psychologists, and educators agree that perhaps 70% of all that programming is achieved by age six and perhaps as much as 95% is completed by age 14. This means that by the mid-teen years much of a person's self-image is set.

Think of the programming that occurred during our formative years. By the mid-teen years, most people have created a "box" about how they perceive themselves. This early programming is likely to become permanent unless we consciously choose to change it later in life. For many of us, this is scary.

Dr. Shad Helmstetter, in his best-selling book, *What to Say When You Talk to Yourself,* offers some shocking statistics about how programming occurs and what type is most prevalent: "During the first 18 years of our lives, if we grew up in fairly average, reasonably positive homes, we were told 'No!,' or what we could *not* do, more than *148,000 times!* If you were a little more fortunate, you may have been told 'No!' only 100,000 times, or 50,000 times—however many, it was considerably more negative programming than any of us needs.

"Meanwhile, during the sample period, the first 18 years

of your life, how often do you suppose you were told what you *can do* or what you *can* accomplish in life? A few thousand times? A few hundred? During my speaking engagements to groups across the country, I have had people tell me they could not remember being told what they *could* accomplish in life more than three or four times! Whatever the number, for most of us the 'yes's' we received simply didn't balance out the 'no's.' The occasional 'words of belief' were just that—occasional—and they were far outweighed by our daily doses of 'cannots.' "

Helmstetter concedes that much of the negative programming was well intentioned. However, he offers this sobering conclusion: "Leading behavioral researchers have told us that as much as 75% of everything we think is negative, counterproductive, and works against us. . . . It's no wonder. What if the researchers are correct? That means that as much as 75% or more of our programming is the wrong kind."

As you were growing up, in what ways were you encouraged?

In what ways were you discouraged?

Were you continually criticized for what you were doing wrong, or were you rewarded or acknowledged for what you were doing right?

As a leader, in what ways can you better encourage your people (and yourself)?

As a result of this conditioning, many people are inclined to look for what is wrong or what is not working rather than for what is right or what is working. It somehow seems encouraging that other people have problems, too. This conditioned orientation toward looking for what is wrong directly affects the collective attitudes of their organizations. As they relate to others from this "what's-wrong" perspective, they tend to threaten the self-images of others. These other organization members are likely to move into a defensive, self-protective mode to avoid being blamed for the problems—a reactive state.

Let's relate this concept to the 80/20 Rule of Thumb. Chances are that 80% or more of the people with whom we work have grown up in a "what's wrong," problem-oriented environment. Many were disciplined more for doing things wrong than rewarded for doing things right. Therefore, a majority, probably 80% or more, have generally negative self-images and will instinctively spend substantial energy on trying to keep others from seeing the weaknesses they perceive in themselves. They sometimes do this by pointing out what's wrong with everything or everyone else. When they find something wrong with someone else or with some situation or circumstance, it takes the focus off their own *perceived* limitations. This is simply the way they are conditioned to protect their own self-esteem. This is the fundamental mindset of Reactive Thinking.

This suggests that as many as 80% or more of the employees who walk into your business every morning have a fundamentally negative orientation. During the day they will tend to naturally look for what's wrong. By focusing on what is wrong with something or someone else, attention is less likely to be focused on what is wrong with themselves. This automatic, usually subconscious, defense mechanism will have them naturally looking for and seeing what's wrong with any new idea, new procedure, or new system we introduce. This orientation is even more predominant in some of the problem-oriented professions such as engineering, accounting, and law where people are *taught* to look for what's wrong or what's not working.

> *Are conversations or meetings with your people primarily about what they are doing wrong or what is working and what you want more of?*

SELF-IMAGE AND PERSONAL PERFORMANCE

To the degree that people have a poor self-image or low self-esteem, the predominance of their attention, at least subconsciously, is focused on what's *wrong with themselves* and how to keep others from seeing their weaknesses. When their focus is inward and specifically on what is wrong with themselves, they are likely to feel threatened by change. They do not want to upset the status quo. They know how to do it the way they have always done it. They know the results they will get by doing it that way, even if those results are not really very impressive. It feels safe doing it the same old way. It does not feel safe doing it a new way. Though they are not happy, they are reasonably "comfortable" in the certainty of the "box" they are in.

No matter how much sense it seems to make logically, a new way is unfamiliar, unpredictable territory to such people. They believe they might not be able to do it, and they might, therefore, look bad and be blamed for the failure. Then, they would feel worse about themselves. To avoid this possibility, they become resistant or reactive. Again, this attitude is formed when the predominance of their attention is focused inward on the less positively perceived aspects of themselves, as in Figure 3. In this mode, their continuous goal, consciously or unconsciously, is to guard against the world seeing their weaknesses. This mode is a self-protective, defensive posture and often shows up as "turf-guarding" and blaming others.

The energy these people waste protecting themselves is energy unavailable for focusing on the organization's needs.

Additionally, the energy they use to protect themselves is unavailable for creating the future—for creating what they want. The degree to which people's energy is drained by trying to protect their self-image is the degree of resistance to change we will experience when trying to get those same people to make a change.

As problems occur or changes are required, self-images that are already negative will be revalidated. Let's look at why this is true. The Reactive Thinkers often see *any* suggested change, even those that make logical sense to them, as a statement that there is something wrong with the way they are already doing things. At a deeper level, they see this as a statement that something is wrong with them personally. Therefore, when someone asks them to change, the request is perceived as someone pointing out a flaw that threatens their already sagging self-esteem. To the degree their self-esteem is threatened or injured, people feel a need to protect themselves.

Many people feel especially defensive when someone challenges the way they are doing something—whatever it is. There is a safety factor in doing it *their* way, the way they've always done it; there is uncertainty in any *new way*, and the uncertainty threatens their feelings of safety. They feel a loss of control, and being in control is very important to a person with low self-esteem. Losing control means the world may find out about "what's wrong with them" as they perceive it. Also, the degree to which they perceive something negative being said about them and the degree to

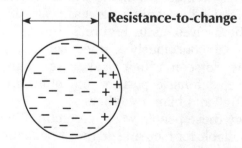

which they react to that perception is directly related to what they really feel deep down is wrong with themselves. The more negatively they perceive themselves, the more reactive or defensive they will be.

Those whose self-esteem is relatively high—the 20%ers/ Creative Thinkers—only have a limited amount of their energy and attention focused on what's wrong with them. They are mostly comfortable with who they are. Their high level of self-esteem usually is reflected by a high level of enthusiasm. Since they don't feel as much need to protect themselves, they can easily turn their focus away from themselves and toward what needs to get done. They are more effectively focused, and the commitment level is higher for what needs to be accomplished.

Creative Thinkers are "can-do" oriented and tend to see change as an opportunity. They waste very little energy on protecting their weaknesses from being discovered; therefore, much more energy is available to apply toward their objectives. So, when asked to make changes, they are less likely to take that request as a statement of personal wrongdoing or of their way not being good enough. They are more likely to accept the change as a new and better way to achieve higher performance. They tend to see changes as a challenge and an opportunity to win. This is the fundamental mindset of Creative Thinking.

Here is another way to look at Reactive and Creative Thinking. In the Chinese language, there are two symbols for our word "crisis." One symbol defines crisis as "danger."

Resistance-to-change

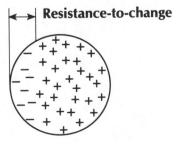

The other symbol defines crisis as "opportunity." The Creative Thinking 20%ers see the opportunity in change and/or crisis. The Reactive 80%ers tend to only see the danger—how they can lose or be hurt—in change or crisis. Both perspectives are valid. Which one we choose to guide us will have a profound effect on what we accomplish.

We often are asked, "Can you change people's attitudes? Can you change the basic way people are?" No, but people *can* change their *own* attitudes. They can change their attitudes and the way they behave to the degree that they *want* to change. More importantly, we as leaders can create an environment that supports enhancing the self-images of our people. As people truly feel better about themselves, their attitudes naturally change for the benefit of all. As people break out of their "boxes" and better understand who they really are—that they are okay just the way they are—they naturally let go of the need to protect themselves. This awakening and personal renewal releases tremendous discretionary energy that can be utilized for the benefit of others. This is a natural growth process that can be expedited dramatically by Enlightened Leadership.

Without the support of Enlightened Leadership in some aspect of their lives, many people who are locked in poor self-image "boxes" are doomed to wait until a personal crisis forces them to look differently at their "victim" perspectives, their non-"response-able" mindsets. The factors we can manage that support the mindset shifts so critical to our personal and organizational success is the focus of the remainder of this book.

Change-Friendly Highlights

1. The 80/20 Rule of Thumb suggests that 20% of your people will be open to change while 80% will be resistant to change to varying degrees.

2. People's perception of themselves and how they believe others perceive them defines their self-esteem/ self-image.

3. Self-esteem is a major factor in people's attitudes. People with low self-esteem may resist change because they interpret it as an indictment of their worth.

4. Reactive Thinkers often see any request for change as a suggestion that something is wrong with them. Creative Thinkers tend to see a request for change as an opportunity and challenge.

The source of all energy, passion, motivation, and an internally generated desire to do good work is our own feeling about what we are doing.

PETER BLOCK
The Empowered Manager

5

LOOKING AT FOCUS

*Success . . . My nomination for the single
most important ingredient is energy well
directed.*

LOUIS B. LUNDBORG
Former Chairman, Bank of America

We Get What We Focus On

Where and how individuals and organizations focus their attention and energy dramatically impacts the results they achieve. Moreover, many of us are naturally distracted from focusing effectively or productively. The focus issue is a soft issue. It often *causes* many of the measurable hard issues encountered in organizations. For this reason, a fundamental mindset issue that leadership must understand and address revolves around focus.

Let's look closer at our ability to focus. The human eye is indeed an amazing organ. When functioning properly, it can detect objects or movements within a full 180-degree periphery. Yet, for all we can see simultaneously, we can focus clearly on only one object at a time.

All day, every day, we continuously shift our focus from one thing to another depending upon what seems most interesting, important, or threatening to us at each instant. If what we see is compelling enough, we direct our energies toward it. When we wish to channel our energies in a different direction, we shift our focus there. We look in the direction we want to walk, at a phrase we wish to read, at a piece of food we'd like to eat, or on a project we need to complete.

The Two Sides of Attention

Just as we direct and focus our eyes, we can choose where to direct our overall mental focus. We also can choose how we will interpret what we see, feel, hear, smell, taste, sense, or if we will pay attention at all. We can, for example, look right at something and not see it, such as when we are daydreaming or have our minds on something other than what is at hand. In addition, our enormous capacity for concentration allows us to focus on one thing to such a degree that everything else fades into oblivion. Thus, we are able to channel our energies into the most productive vein at any given moment.

Jerry Rice, outstanding pass receiver for the Super Bowl Champion San Francisco 49ers, uses this ability to his benefit. He says that when he goes out for a pass, all he thinks about is seeing the ball come into his hands. Once the ball is safely in his hands, all he sees is the goal line. Currently, he is on track to break virtually every NFL receiving record by a wide margin.

This ability to concentrate—to focus all of our physical and mental energy on one thing—is like a two-edged sword. Sometimes we get so caught up in paying attention to a distraction, real or imagined, that we don't focus on what really matters. "Fixation" is what psychologists call extreme cases of this concept.

Have you ever been driving down the road so mentally distracted that you missed your turn or didn't see a stoplight? Then, you know what we mean.

To see a different way this concept works, think back to the last time you bought a new car. Remember finally picking the exact make, model, and color you wanted? Then what happened? Did it seem like you saw cars everywhere just like the one you bought? If so, the reason for this is simple. The other cars were out there all along, but you did not notice them. When the specific automobile type became fixed in your mind, your attention automatically was drawn to similar automobiles.

A MODEL FOR FOCUSING ENERGY

This leads us to an important concept: We naturally become fixated on, attract more of, or move toward that upon which we focus our attention. The power of a clear goal, for example, is that it provides a focal point for our attention and energy, thus helping us move toward it.

During a discussion of the focus issue, the comptroller for a company in Texas offered a practical observation: "When I was a kid, I would ride my bike to the swimming hole, and my attention would be focused on all the fun I was going to have and on seeing my friends. As I'd ride along and see a big rock on the path, I'd notice it and automatically see what I needed to do to get around it and zip on down the path. My mind would be so focused on getting to the swimming hole and on the fun I would have there that the rocks along the way were not reasons I could not get there, just obstacles to address and get by.

"I remember once, I saw a rock in my path no larger than the others, but this time I stared at it and my front tire smacked right into it. I sprawled on the ground. My focus shifted from 'getting to the swimming hole' to the 'rock on the path.' Focusing on the obstacle stopped my progress toward my goal."

While the analogy seems rather simple, so are the points we want to make. They are:

(1) We tend to move *toward* what we focus our attention on.

(2) When we focus our energy on the obstacles in our path, we spend time and energy dealing with those obstacles rather than on getting where we want to go.

(3) When we are clearly focused on where we want to go, we do whatever we need to do to get there with minimal wasted energy.

In this book, we will use the graphic on page 79 as a model of the choices we have about where we can focus our attention and energy—a focus model, or model of choices. The words on each side of the model will change depending on the situation. For example, for the previous story about riding the bicycle to the swimming hole, the cyclist had a choice of focusing on where he wanted to go or on the obstacles in his path. The model of the choices would look like the diagram on the following page.

We have a choice. We can either focus our attention and

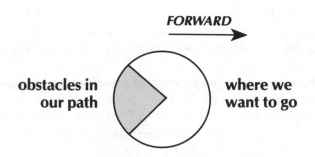

energy on the obstacles in our path or on where we want to go. Only one of these choices leads us to where we want to go. We achieve or receive what we focus upon. The model suggests the desired focus is on the "Forward," or right side.

To the extent we focus on the forward side of the focus model, we move closer to where we want to go. Creative Thinkers tend to focus most of their energy on "where we want to go" and get there much quicker as a result. Reactive Thinkers tend to focus more of their energy on the "obstacles" side of the model. To the extent we focus on the obstacles in our path, we are held back from getting to where we want to go.

> *What* situations can you think of in your or-
> ganization in which people may be so focused
> on all of the problems that they may have lost
> sight of the original objective? *Credits*
>
> *What* situations can you think of in which
> people were so focused on what they wanted
> to achieve that they overcame any obstacles
> to achieve the goal? *Food Show/*

Often the most and best energy of an organization's people gets so focused on the reasons why they cannot obtain the results they want that little energy is available for focusing on what needs to be done to achieve those results. The model of these choices would look like the diagram below.

If our people are more focused on all the reasons why they cannot achieve goals, they are indeed likely to miss the mark. To the extent they are focused on the desired results and what needs to be one to achieve them, they will progress effectively toward those results.

Misdirected focusing goes on every day to varying degrees in many organizations, and everyone from front-line employees to top executives contributes to this issue. Based on their conditioning, the default focus for the 80%ers/ Reactive Thinkers in particular tends to be on the reasons they cannot achieve something.

Many of our people are unable or unwilling to make conscious choices about where they focus their attention. As leaders, we have an opportunity to refocus our people for their good as well as for the good of the organization.

Often people simply are not aware of the choices they have about the direction of their focus. In *Conflict Management . . . The Courage to Confront,* Richard J. Mayer explains it this way: "We each create our own separate reality. One way we do so is by selecting what we experience. We can effectively pay attention to only one thing at a time. So, we turn down the car radio when we look to find the number of the house we've never visited; we turn off the television while we memorize a

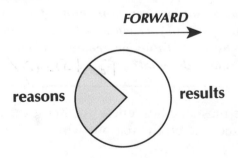

poem. We cannot hold a conversation and read at the same time.

"We pick out what we choose to be aware of from an ocean of possibilities. If you are on the road and hungry, you see restaurants and little else; if you break off the heel of your shoe, the shoe repair shop stands out and the rest of your surroundings (including the restaurants) fade into the background. If you perceive so-and-so to be untrustworthy, you notice only evidence that agrees with your perception. You somehow hear just your own name across a noisy room.

"We see what we want or desire to see, we choose what we are aware of—sometimes whether or not it's there," says Mayer.

Both individuals and organizations have a choice as to where energy or attention is directed. A person or an entire team can greatly impact results achieved by making conscious choices about where attention is focused. If we focus on what we want more of, positive results are increased, because selecting something to focus upon tends to draw more and more of it to us.

Consider the most critical issues faced by your organization. Is the predominant focus on the objective and what needs to be done to achieve it, or is the focus on what's wrong with the current status or all the reasons the team or organization cannot achieve the objective?

What benefits could you reap if the focus could be shifted so that more of the attention was on solutions?

The vice president of sales for a medium-sized computer company in the Northeast had a difficult situation. His 250-

person organization had been downsized twice during the previous six months, and people were frustrated, upset, and hostile. As a result, sales had decreased. He decided to have a national sales meeting and knew that success of this strategic meeting would be critical to the organization's ability to turn the sales momentum around. For this reason, he took on the responsibility of kicking off the two-day session himself.

As he began the session, the tension was so great that it felt as if the auditorium could explode at any moment from the hostility. During his one-hour opening session, however, something amazing happened. By totally focusing on the *positive* aspects of the previous six months, he shifted the attitudes of the people so dramatically that at the end of his hour he received a standing ovation. At the next break, he heard appreciation from many people who were optimistic about their future. More importantly, the overall meeting was a rousing success and was crucial to the beginning of their turnaround.

There are focus choices to make every moment of every day. In each situation, we can choose between focusing on what *is* working and what we want more of, or we can concentrate our attention on analyzing what is *not* working, what we don't want—either way we get more of whatever we focus on.

WE ATTRACT WHAT WE TRY TO AVOID

Another key issue with respect to focus concerns how much energy we put into avoiding a certain situation or problem. Just as focusing on what we want more of tends to draw us closer to it and bring more of it into our experience, the attention and energy we put into trying to avoid something tends to draw us closer to it as well.

We already saw this concept illustrated by the story of the boy riding his bike to the swimming hole. When he shifted his focus to "avoiding rocks," he hit the rock he wanted to avoid and wrecked his bike. Here's another simple example of how this principle works. Take a moment to imagine a beautiful, sandy beach. Now, just for a few moments, do not think of that beautiful, sandy beach. Avoid thinking of the beautiful, sandy beach. What happened? Were you able to avoid thinking of the beach? Probably not.

By trying *not* to focus on something, which is the same as avoiding focusing on it, we actually focus all our attention in its direction. Thus, *avoiding* something doesn't work. If you were successful in not thinking of the beach, how did you do it? In all likelihood, by focusing on something entirely different than a beautiful, sandy beach. In other words, the only way we can change our focus from what we want to avoid is to replace it with something else we *want* to focus upon. You might have focused on a car, on food, on a person—anything to *replace* the beach.

So, where is our attention focused when we are trying to avoid, for example, mistakes? Our attention is on the very mistakes we want to avoid! With our attention on mistakes, we are likely to make more of them. Avoiding doesn't work! If we want to minimize mistakes, we must focus on what we *do* want, not what we don't want. What we *want* is accuracy or effectiveness or whatever is the opposite of what we want to avoid. A generic focus model would look like the diagram on page 84. The model suggests the importance of focusing on what we *do* want, not what we don't want.

Warren Bennis and Bert Nanus explored this concept in depth in their book *Leaders: The Strategies for Taking Charge* through the story of Karl Wallenda. During April 1978, Karl Wallenda, the 73-year-old patriarch of one of history's greatest tightrope-walking families, was booked to do a series of breathtaking solo walks on a high wire stretched between two beach-front hotels in San Juan, Puerto Rico. As hundreds of spectators watched, the master

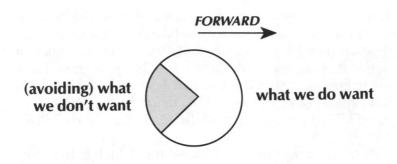

began moving carefully on the 120-foot-high cable with the same dazzling dexterity he had shown thousands of times before. This time, however, halfway across the cable Wallenda suddenly lost his balance, plunged to the ground, and was killed instantly.

As the media and his family later analyzed what had happened, one distinct trend surfaced—Wallenda was focusing on what he wanted to avoid. The model of choices he had for where to focus his attention would look like the diagram below.

Karl's widow explained: "All Karl thought about for three straight months prior [to the event] was *falling*. It was the first time he'd ever thought about that, and it seemed to me that he put all his energies into *not falling* rather than walking the tightrope." Mrs. Wallenda added that he had even taken great pains to personally supervise installation

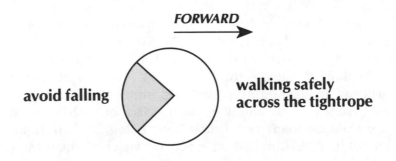

of the guy wires holding the tightrope between the hotels, something "he had never even thought of doing before." Where Wallenda had always been keenly intent on his goal—walking safely across the wire—his focus in this instance had shifted to not falling.

This story provides a tragic example of how negative focusing can pull us toward an outcome we're trying to avoid. Some of us have been taught this principle as it relates to life-and-death situations in the world. For example, we know that if we focus upon oncoming car headlights when driving at night we may have a head-on collision, and if we look at objects, such as power lines, in our path when hang gliding or parachuting we are likely to fly right into them. Or, if we stare at the car beside us in traffic, we are likely to move toward it. We must shift our attention to where we *want* to go or what we *want* to create, not on what we want to avoid.

This principle applies equally well to what can become life-and-death situations in the corporate world. For example, where is our attention when we are focused on zero defects? When we are focused on zero defects, we are focused on *defects*, and we are likely to have more of them. Our model of choices that suggests the appropriate direction for our focus would look like the diagram below.

The organizations that produce the highest quality are focused on seeing how close they can get to 100% yield in parts, assemblies, service, or whatever. They are not fo-

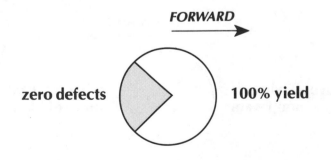

cused on zero defects. Of course, as they create better and better yield, they do indeed approach zero defects, but not by focusing on them.

(*Note:* It is our experience that *some* short-term success can be achieved by focusing on zero defects *if* defects are very high. To achieve extraordinary long-term reduction in defects, however, requires a shift in focus to improving yield.)

An example of this was a manufacturing firm we worked with in New York. Management had tried various approaches to "reduce scrap" below 8% and had used charts that recorded their progress by plotting percentage of scrap. Over and over, they were frustrated in their attempts.

After beginning to manage the focus of their people and move it toward what they wanted more of instead of what they didn't want, management changed the parameters on the charts they were using. Instead of measuring percentage of scrap, they began measuring percentage of good parts (% yield) produced. When people's focus shifted from what they *wanted more of,* instead of what they *did not want,* good parts were increased 2% in only six weeks. This slight increase in yield translated into a reduction in scrap of 25%! The only thing that changed was what they focused on.

Another way of seeing this model of choices is shown in the diagram below.

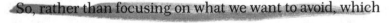

So, rather than focusing on what we want to avoid, which

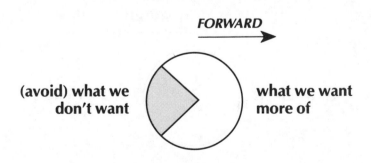

FORWARD

(avoid) what we
don't want

what we want
more of

obviously poses some hazards, we must learn to focus our
attention in a more effective direction—on what we want
more of or on our goal. In the approaching headlight example, we choose to focus on our side of the road. In the
hang-glider example, we focus on exactly where we want
to fly or land. In traffic we focus on our own lane, in business we focus on our goals, our objectives, our mission, our
vision of where we want to be. We need focus targets to
move toward.

---

*When was your organization being distracted
from its mission by trying to avoid something?*

*On the other side of the equation, what ob-
stacles have you overcome recently by keeping focused on what you want to accomplish?*

Remember, however, that it is important to reset our focus
continually. It is natural for day-to-day problems and other
distractions to pull us off the desired focus. For example,
an airline crew flying from New York to San Francisco
continually checks on the plane's position and resets its
course. For only a small percentage of the trip is the plane
actually right on course, but by keeping focused on the
destination, it is a simple matter for the crew to check its
position and correct the plane's course as needed. By checking and correcting frequently, they need to make only minor
adjustments.

No matter what we are doing or where we are going,
deviations from the desired course will occur. By staying
focused on the objective, however, it is simple for us to make
corrections and do what is necessary to move closer to our
goal.

PROBLEM VS. SOLUTIONS ORIENTATION

At times, organizational problems loom so large that it seems almost impossible to focus on the solutions we want to achieve rather than on the problems themselves. Yet, the differences between the two approaches are dramatic.

A problem orientation:

- **Puts a spotlight on what is not working—on what is wrong**

- **Looks for someone to blame**

- **Causes defensiveness**

- **Stifles creativity**

- **Causes more problems as attention is drawn to the problems that already exist**

- **Drains off valuable energy**

- **Keeps us stuck in boxes**

Many organizations tend toward a problem orientation because most individuals in them have a natural inclination to focus on what is wrong or on what is not working. This tendency goes all the way back to our early conditioning and our self-image. It gets us mired down in the problems themselves. Subsequently, the energy we focus on problems reduces the amount of energy available to apply to achieving the results we want or to creating the solutions we need.

When we center our attention on any problem, all of our energy gets focused on that problem. In the process, we may only see the problem and may neglect other things that need our attention. For one, we may be so mired in the problem we may miss seeing the solution.

> *Think of what happens when people have distracting personal problems. How does this affect their work performance?*
>
> *When people are distracted by work-related problems, how does this affect the energy they put into their job objectives? How does this affect the results they get?*
>
> *What is this effect on people's performance costing your organization in wasted time? In productivity? In stress?*

On the other hand, a solution orientation:

- Puts the spotlight on strengthening what is already working

- Develops openness and involvement

- Naturally moves us toward the goal it is focused upon

- Creates energy and enthusiasm

- Creates open communication and continuous renewal

- Develops the atmosphere best suited for generating creative solutions

Ed tells this account of an experience he had that highlights this point: "One day while we were working on this chapter, I went out jogging. I was thinking about how to best get these focus concepts across. My usual course takes me down a well-worn footpath by a stream. As I neared a particular segment of the path, I began to dread what was ahead. One short section of the path is covered with a thick layer of loose sand. It is difficult to run through, slows me down, creates the possibility of twisting an ankle, and forces me to break my stride. The thought of running on this part of the path always sapped my energy.

"This particular day, I was suddenly aware of my mindset around the issue and realized I could choose to look at it differently. I realized a more appropriate objective than to avoid getting hurt or slowing down might be to see how easily and safely I could navigate this part of the path. Instead of focusing on all the problems with the sand, I knew I could focus on a new objective instead. As soon as I focused on this new objective, I noticed something. On the right edge of the path was an area where the sand was not as thick. Of the numerous times I had jogged this trail, I had never seen this before. I took this right edge route. It was easy, safe, and didn't slow me down or break my stride—and I was energized by the discovery.

"In the past, I had been so mired in the problem of the sand that I could not see the seemingly obvious solution. By simply shifting my attention to the results I wanted, the solution appeared instantly."

All of us run into sand traps on the road of life, but the successful people and organizations we encounter look upon these situations not as problems in which to get mired but as challenges or opportunities—things that need to be handled on the way to the end result. They keep their focus on the objective, and with this focus they are more easily

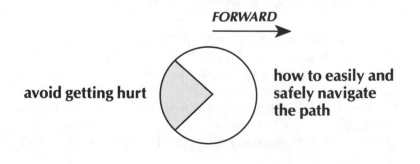

able to come up with solutions to the problems they encounter. They certainly spend time looking at and understanding the problem. But they spend very little time on the problem itself. They quickly shift their attention to the solution side. This is a subtle, yet very strategic, difference in the mindset.

Failure to understand the subtle distinction between focusing on *what is wrong with where we are* instead of on *what will it take to get to where we want to be* costs organizations dearly. The losses show up in: poor quality, lower productivity, higher costs, increased stress levels, embittered relationships (often at times when cooperation is most essential), lowered levels of trust and cooperation, untimely loss of key people, and strained customer relations—all of which show up on the bottom line as lost profits.

It is important to note that the fundamental focus principle is not about ignoring problems or pretending they do not exist. It is about dealing with problems as they arise without letting them bog us down. It is about staying focused on what we want to achieve. It is the difference between looking at *what is wrong with where we are now* (energy focused on the past) and looking at *what needs to be done to get to where we want to be* (energy focused on creating the future from where we are now). This subtle shift in focus puts most of our energy into finding solutions instead of into getting mired in the problem. The model of the choices would be:

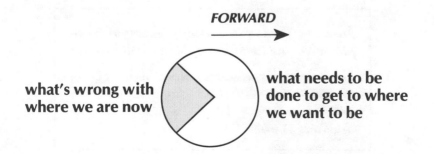

FORWARD

what's wrong with where we are now

what needs to be done to get to where we want to be

> *How* much more effective would your organization be if more of your people approached their work by focusing on the desired results consistently rather than focusing on the problems or reasons they cannot achieve the results?
>
> *Where* in your organization could you have the most immediate impact by shifting where your people are focusing their attention? *At System*
>
> *What* would be the benefits to your team when the shift is made? To the organization as a whole? For you personally?
>
> *What* is one thing you could do today to begin causing that shift to take place? *open environment*

Internalizing this focus concept is essential to making the mindset shift required to become a continually renewing person or organization. Enlightened Leaders understand that this is a subtle but significant shift and that it is critical to moving people beyond their resistance. It also may be vital to your organization's very survival and success. The next chapter provides a framework for creating this critical mindset shift.

> *In* what ways do you already support your people in staying focused on the desired results?
>
> *Knowing* that our culture tends to pull us into the problem orientation, what can you do to get your people back on the solutions-orientation track?

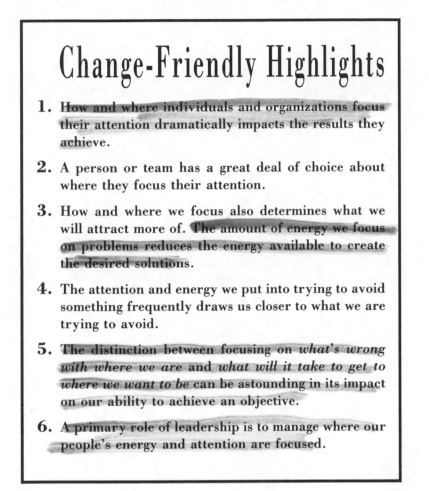

Change-Friendly Highlights

1. How and where individuals and organizations focus their attention dramatically impacts the results they achieve.

2. A person or team has a great deal of choice about where they focus their attention.

3. How and where we focus also determines what we will attract more of. The amount of energy we focus on problems reduces the energy available to create the desired solutions.

4. The attention and energy we put into trying to avoid something frequently draws us closer to what we are trying to avoid.

5. The distinction between focusing on *what's wrong with where we are* and *what will it take to get to where we want to be* can be astounding in its impact on our ability to achieve an objective.

6. A primary role of leadership is to manage where our people's energy and attention are focused.

It is a process of diverting one's scattered forces into one powerful channel.

JAMES ALLEN

6

GENERATING THE MINDSET SHIFT

No great improvements in the lot of man-kind are possible until a great change takes place in the fundamental constitution of their modes of thought.

JOHN STUART MILL
English Economist and Philosopher
(1806—73)

THE NEW PARADIGM

The most effective and successful leaders in today's dynamic business environment are those who have already discovered the *key to renewal*—creating a major shift in their people's mindsets from one that keeps them stuck in boxes to one that naturally searches for new and innovative solutions. For an organization to embark on the journey of renewal, its people must move beyond the natural resistance-to-change mode and move toward the highly focused, strategic, productive, empowered mindset of Creative Thinking—the 20%ers. This shifting of the individual and collective mindsets is, in fact, the solution to unlocking the energy, creativity, vitality, and spirit of people, teams, and organizations.

The best-performing organizations achieve the highest levels of both organizational results and human satisfaction concurrently. To accomplish this, they must first develop a new framework, or a new paradigm, that emphasizes fundamental yet frequently neglected components of personal and organizational effectiveness. These components include personal empowerment, energy management, quality consciousness, clear purpose, inspiring vision, and alignment. This paradigm requires the development of new approaches that directly address the real issue: the need to manage the collective mindset or attitude of the people.

Primary importance is given to these renewal factors; and traditional factors, such as cost containment, quality improvement, higher productivity, increased sales, enhanced customer service, and increasing profitability become secondary concerns. Improvement in these hard measures are seen as the *results* of how well leaders are managing the soft people issues, including how well they are focusing their people's attention and energy.

SHIFTING PARADIGMS

The word "paradigm" has a rich heritage that evolved through the Greek, Latin, and French languages. It is defined as a pattern, example, or model. Contemporary behaviorists and sociologists use this word to describe any idea or set of ideas that provides the basis for a framework of beliefs and actions. Simply put, a paradigm is a controlling perception—a mindset.

Each of us sees the world from within a number of different paradigms. However, our paradigms change, and even our once tightly held controlling perceptions can shift over time. For example, a once commonly held paradigm is "The world is flat." Nearly everyone believed this until 1492. "It is not possible to put a man on the moon" is a paradigm that people held for centuries. Until the 1960s most thought it impossible, but the refutation of this paradigm was broadcast to the world during 1969. "Smoking is an individual right" is a paradigm that only recently changed for a large portion of the Western world. For many years, smokers could light a cigarette anywhere or anytime they wanted. Beginning in 1990, airlines banned all smoking on North American continental flights, and a growing number of restaurants now have large no-smoking sections or have prohibited smoking altogether in their establishments.

We shift a variety of paradigms numerous times throughout our lives. For example, we do so when we learn to do something new, like learning to ride a bicycle or work on a computer. Long before we learn to ride a bike, we know intellectually what we need to do. We know we need to pedal to keep the bike moving. We know we must turn the handle bars to keep the bike balanced and moving in the right direction. Regardless of what we know "intellectually," most of us fall over many times as we actually learn to ride. Then, seemingly in an instant, it all comes together, and we successfully ride the bicycle. A shift takes place inside us, and suddenly we really *know* how to ride the bike. We have just experienced a paradigm shift. Once that shift has occurred, we will always know how to ride a bike.

In much the same way, when first learning to use a computer we feel clumsy, but the more we learn about and work with the machine, the more a shift begins to take place. The shift may be sudden or it may be gradual. Either way, a paradigm shift occurs when we internalize the knowledge. At this point, it becomes more than an intellectual understanding. When the shift does come, sitting down to work on a computer becomes easy. The actions required become automatic, and we no longer have to think too much about what we are doing. We do it naturally.

Yet some paradigms are difficult to change. Many business organizations are locked into old paradigms that are ineffective and costly. It seems easier to stay locked in old, known, comfortable boxes. Continuous renewal, however, can only be achieved by organizations and individuals who

> *Where in your organization may people be doing things one way just because they always did them that way?*
>
> *What paradigms is your team or organization operating from that may be limiting your ability to achieve your objectives? What is it costing? What needs to change?*
>
> *What paradigms about management exist that may be limiting your organization? What does management do that tends to perpetuate those limiting paradigms?*
>
> *What one thing can you do differently today to help your people make the essential shift in paradigms?*

are willing to undergo shifts in thinking—to re-examine their paradigms and find ways out of their boxes. Continuous renewal requires that we stop doing things the way we've always done them just because that's how we've *always* done them.

PERSONAL PARADIGMS

Whatever your organization's stage of development, everyone brings to it their own collection of paradigms—beliefs. Dr. Carl Sorensen, a professor at Stanford University, says, "There's an old expression, 'Seeing is believing.' But it's more accurate to say that 'believing is seeing.' That is, you tend to see what you believe you're going to see. You bring to a situation what you expect you're going to experience."

If we go to a party believing we are not going to have a good time, we will look for and find plenty of reasons to support our belief. We will notice some people standing around bored, someone upset about something, or someone in a bad mood. We will actually subconsciously seek to prove through our experience of the party that we were right about not having a good time. Our mind likes to be right. Unless we somehow shift our state of mind, we can count on not having a good time. What we focus on, based on the decision we made even before the party, is what we will experience.

On the other hand, if we go to the party with the expectation that we are going to have a good time, we will look for and notice plenty of situations that support that belief. We will see the people who are laughing and talking and dancing, or people who are happy and enjoying themselves. Our experience of the party is dependent upon the expectations we have about it. And, yes, both these scenarios are the same party!

To see how this concept works in the business arena, we'll use one of our clients as an example. We worked with a company in New York that had a long history of strikes and grievances. It was an especially interesting workshop, because both management and union officers participated. The tension in the room was thick. Many of the people were second- and third-generation union members.

The union members saw management from one particular paradigm: they thought that all managers wanted to do was to see how much they could get out of workers while paying them as little as possible. The management team had similar limitations in its paradigm: they saw the union as wanting to do as little work as possible while getting paid as much as possible. Both groups were locked in their old paradigms, unable to see any other perspective.

During the workshop process, however, something began to happen. A new level of trust began to develop. People began opening up to each other and tension began easing. People from both groups started interacting and a higher level of communication and understanding developed. A shift in mindsets spread until at one point the union president stood up and declared, "The wall between union and management is officially down. We need to be looking at how we can work together in a way to help our company assure the future for all of us."

The paradigm shift of the individuals participating in the workshop from a hostile "we-versus-them" to an "it's-all-us" mindset was astounding, and later the culture of the entire organization experienced the same shift. The company went on to set new standards for productivity

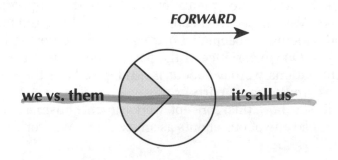

and finished the year with the highest annual profit in their history. All this occurred while the relationship between union members and management turned around dramatically.

> *Where might the "we-versus-them" paradigm be costing your organization?*
>
> *What would be the benefits to your organization of moving from a "we-versus-them" mindset to an "it's-all-us" attitude?*
>
> *In what ways could you lead this shift?*

THE POWER OF SHIFTING FOCUS

We've observed some truly exciting things happen when enough people in organizations make the paradigm shift away from a problem orientation to a solution orientation. For instance, a major computer company had taken on an enormous software development project. It was a complex undertaking involving hundreds of people and was contracted to be delivered in 48 months.

Well into the project it became clear to top management that it would take 18 months longer than originally scheduled to deliver the software to the customer. The ax hanging over the head of every employee was a penalty for tens of millions of dollars to be assessed if the venture was even one day late. It was seen as such an impossible situation that management had virtually written off the huge penalty as a foregone conclusion and were more concerned about operating expenses for the extra 18 months. They were clearly stuck in a paradigm that said they were so far behind schedule that there was no hope of catching up. All they could see was what was wrong with their situation, the problems they faced.

Despite this environment, there was an incredible turn-around. With only 10 months left the project went from being 18 months behind schedule to completion 30 days ahead of the original deadline. The difference was not a new invention or a technological breakthrough but a major mindset shift—a paradigm shift in focus. Instead of focusing on all the reasons they were 18 months behind schedule, the people were empowered to shift their focus toward what needed to happen to achieve the original objective. The focus model looks like the diagram below.

The people had been so enmeshed in all the problems, all the reasons they were so far behind schedule, they had lost sight of the original goal—to deliver quality software on time. The mandate driven down from top management was to find out what was wrong so it could be fixed. This diverted people's focus from getting the job done (their original objective), to finding the cause of the delay and avoiding getting blamed for the problems.

As the project got further and further behind, the drive from the top became stronger and stronger to find what was wrong and place blame for the problems. Trust and cooperation diminished from the frequent finger pointing and resultant conflicts. Defensive postures abounded. At a time when it was most crucial for the people to work together as a team, they were driven even further apart by management's incessant quest to hold someone responsible for the situation.

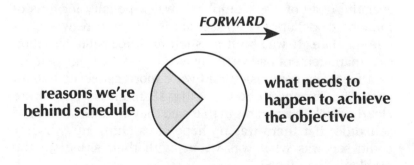

So much of the people's time and energy was going into nonproductive or even counterproductive activity that there was little left over to apply to finding solutions. In this mode of thinking, the creativity of the people was squelched. As more and more energy was spent trying to avoid being blamed for the problems, this defensive energy further reduced what was available for creating the desired results.

Where have you experienced a similar problem orientation that squelched the energy and creativity of your people?

What was the environment like? What were the attitudes of the people?

How was performance impacted? What was the cost in terms of stress?

Through a revitalizing workshop process, as well as insightful leadership, a critical mass of the people made a paradigm shift in their focus. They shifted much of the energy they had been spending on worrying about all the problems to simply focusing on what needed to be done to achieve the objective.

(*Note:* While it is important to understand how this shift was made, right now we would like to look solely at its effects. We will discuss how to create a similar shift later in this chapter.)

This example reveals the enormous amounts of untapped potential and discretionary energy available once a shift in thinking and focus occurs. Tremendous productive energy and creativity are freed when members of any team or organization begin to manage better where and how they focus their attention.

Organizations that already have achieved a paradigm

shift in attitude by learning how to better manage the focus of their people's attention are creating a new vision of how teams of people can work together. They are enjoying exciting levels of performance, achievement, and satisfaction that are moving closer and closer to their vision of how good it can be.

NET FORWARD ENERGY ENHANCING RATIO®

When they first begin work, most individuals, teams, and organizations are clearly focused on their objectives. To a great degree, how well those objectives are achieved is determined by the *direct* energy put into them. Direct energy means not just *how much* energy but *how well* that energy is *focused, managed,* and *expended.*

At any given time, we have a certain amount of energy available to us. This is true for individuals, teams, and organizations as a whole. On an ongoing basis, we have choices about how we use the energy available, including our discretionary energy. All of this energy can be used to either move toward or away from the objective.

We refer to the ratio between the productive energy utilized to move us toward our objective and the non- or counterproductive energy that is holding us back as the Net *Forward* Energy Ratio. This mathematical model illustrates the impact on performance of the collective or individual focus of our energy. It assumes we could somehow actually measure our energy utilization.

To use the software development project as an example, let's say that when they were 18 months behind schedule with only 10 months to go, 40% of their time and energy was spent in figuring out what was wrong, who was to blame, and all the reasons they couldn't get done on time. Consequently, only 60% of the available energy was then left over to apply toward the solutions that would enable them to reach the original objective. The Net Forward Energy Ratio model would look like the first diagram below.

When management discovered how to manage the organizational energy more effectively, let's say that they were able to shift an additional 20% of the total energy away from the reasons that they could not achieve their objectives. That additional energy was then refocused on the results they wanted, and the numbers in the model change accordingly, as in the second diagram below.

The Net Forward Energy Ratio in this example shifts from 60 divided by 40, or 1.5, to 80 divided by 20, or 4.0. The shift from 1.5 to 4.0 is almost *triple* the initial Net Forward Energy Ratio, which we see as directly proportional to performance improvement.

That represents a tremendous increase in forward motion, or improved performance, with a relatively small shift

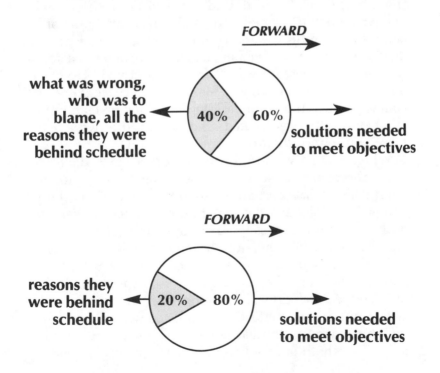

in energy or focus. It was enough of an improvement in performance to go from 18 months behind schedule with only 10 months to deadline to finishing one month ahead of schedule and saving a huge monetary penalty.

Again, we are not proposing that problems be ignored. When we approach what we are doing from a strategic way of thinking that focuses clearly on the desired end result rather than avoiding the problems, we more effectively deal with the real issues that keep us from achieving our goal. We enable ourselves to look at the problems from a perspective that invites solutions rather than one that seeks to place blame.

When our friend Gary showed up at a hotel to conduct a seminar, he found a mistake had been made in bookings and the meeting room was actually being used by someone else. He had a choice at that point. He could work his way through the hotel staff to find out who made the mistake and why it had happened—the problem orientation—or he could focus on his desired result—finding a place to conduct the seminar. We happened to be there and must admit that our first *reaction* was "Who screwed up?" He chose instead to spend his energy looking for a place where he could conduct the seminar. Within a matter of minutes another facility was located, and he and the participants moved on toward their objective.

When we first walk into a meeting room to lead a workshop, there may be a number of things wrong with the room. One choice we have is to find and fix all the things wrong or to look at what we are there to accomplish and deal only with those issues keeping us from our objective. For instance, a light bulb may be out in a light fixture, there may be a tear in the carpet, or the draping on the tables may not be even. We could go through the room with a fine-tooth comb fixing all the things that are wrong. All the energy put in to that effort is a drain, and we could probably find things wrong for the rest of the day. On the other hand, if the light bulb over our flip chart is out, it is important that it be replaced so people can clearly see the charts. The question is, "What needs to be done to get us to where we want to be?" We do not want to put energy into anything not on our list of needs.

Ed tells this story: "I am the primary 'computer person' in our organization, and several years ago we received a new revision of the page-layout software we utilize to create workbooks and marketing materials. I was eager to convert our workbooks to the new software, so I dropped everything I was doing to install the new revision. Besides, I enjoy working with the computer.

"Having installed the software, I began the simple process of automatically converting the 80-page workbook. After the system ground away for about five minutes, it suddenly bombed. System failure! It could not convert! I played around with it for over an hour trying to figure out what I was doing wrong, but kept having the system crash. I finally called the software publisher, and it didn't take them long to tell me our workbook was *not convertible* because of something we had done in the process of creating it. I was upset and frustrated to say the least! The only alternative we had was to convert the workbook manually, one page at a time, which I estimated to be a three- or four-day process of tedious computer work.

"Still upset, I decided I might as well get the project over with and started to work on it. About that time, after I had invested approximately three hours on this minor disaster, Doug came into my office, and I told him what I was doing. After listening to my 'bad-news' story, he asked a simple question: 'How does this project relate to our primary objective?' That question stopped me in my tracks.

"This event occurred when the business was still in a start-up phase. We really had only one objective at the time—sales! Unless we were successful in selling our services, nothing else really mattered. Yet, look how easily I was distracted from our one key objective. The choice model that fits here might look like the diagram on page 108.

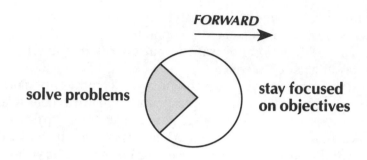

"Was the need to manually convert the workbook to the new software a real problem? Yes, it was. Would converting the workbook support us in accomplishing our immediate objective? Absolutely not! There was nothing wrong with the old version; it served our needs just fine at the time. Eventually, if the software were no longer supported and we had a problem, it could be a critical issue. At this point in our company's development, however, the only things we could really afford to work on were those directly related to selling our services."

The only problems we need to handle are the ones that show up on the way to achieving our critical objectives. And when they do show up, we need to deal with them directly while keeping one eye on the objective and making sure what we are doing moves us closer to that objective. In the computer example, manually converting the workbook to the new software version would have contributed nothing to our critical objective of selling our services.

As leaders learn to better manage energy by shifting their people's focus, a paradigm shift begins to occur throughout their organizations. When a critical mass of people are focused on what they are trying to accomplish and have a "can-do" attitude, instead of a "can't-get-there-from-here" attitude, the impact on performance is profound. People clearly sense the difference. The difference is revitalizing, re-energizing, renewing. It is a shift from the fundamental paradigm of Reactive Thinking to the fundamental paradigm of Creative Thinking (see Chapter 4, page 59). This empowering shift is the key to creating and maintaining a continuous renewal consciousness throughout an organization.

In what ways could you better focus your people's energy toward the results you want?

When things get off track, how could you continually bring them back on track?

What would be the effect on performance to be able to do this consistently?

Consider the diffused power of a 100-watt light bulb. Properly used and strategically placed, it can be very useful. It can illuminate a hallway, or it can light up a backyard. Light bulbs can be used to help a surgeon see clearly during a delicate operation. Yet, if that same amount of light energy is highly focused into a laser beam, it becomes powerful enough to cut through metal. Likewise, the power of focusing an organization's energy like a laser is awesome. It shows up dramatically in results achieved. Is the Net Forward Energy Ratio concept mathematically accurate? We do not know scientifically, but from our experience it fits the real world quite well. In any case, it is a valuable conceptual model.

The key is to focus as much energy as possible in the direction we want to move, which is toward our objective. We can choose to focus our energy like a laser beam in a concentrated, productive direction, or we can diffuse it in any number of directions, some of which are nonproductive or even counterproductive. The model of choices would look like the diagram on page 110.

FORWARD
→

diffused energy concentrated focus

NET FORWARD ENERGY RATIO PERFORMANCE CURVE

Let's look at Net Forward Energy Ratio from the reverse perspective. Suppose we are running a well-focused organization. Our energy is mostly forward-focused and our Net Forward Energy Ratio is high. The choice model we might utilize is shown on page 111.

In this scenario, what would happen if we were suddenly surprised by some bad news?

How would our Net Forward Energy Ratio be affected?

What is the extent of the impact of a small bad-news distraction?

If we plot Net Forward Energy Ratio versus the percentage of energy that is forward-focused, we get the graph on page 111. Let's suppose your organization is on a roll and has 90% of its energy and attention focused on the forward side of the focus model.

The Net Forward Energy Ratio on the graph is forward-focused energy percentage divided by backward-focused

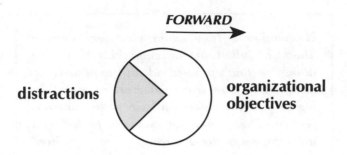

energy percentage, which for this case is $^{90\%}/_{10\%} = 9$. What happens if something occurs that causes the forward focus to drop only 10%? Then, the backward focus increases by 10%, and the Ratio becomes $^{80\%}/_{20\%} = 4$. With only a 10% shift in forward focus, the Net Forward Energy Ratio drops from 9 to 4, to less than half! A slight change in forward focus dramatically impacts our performance.

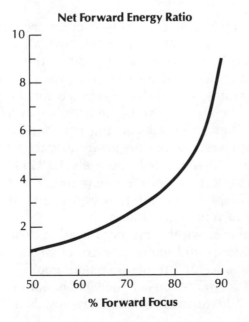

Remember a time when you were moving ahead at full steam on something you were doing, feeling empowered and experiencing satisfaction from what you were accomplishing as you got closer and closer to your objective. Then someone came in to tell you what you were doing wrong. What happened to your productive energy level?

How long did it take to lose your enthusiasm?

How long did it take to build your momentum back up to where it had been?

In remembering how long it took you to rebuild your enthusiasm, what might be the impact on an organization when its people are in a "what's-wrong" mode?

Unfortunately, it is easy to impact an organization in a negative way. All it takes to cause a negative focus shift within an organization or team is a dip in the stock market, takeover talks, downsizings or layoffs, reorganizations, rising interest rates, a breakthrough by a competitor, business closings in the area, or even a negative supervisor or team member. When these concerning situations occur, many people in the organization begin looking for what's wrong with the condition and ask themselves, "How am I going to be hurt by this?" Knowing how much a team can be affected is helpful in seeing how important it is to manage the energy of your organization.

Once people within an organization learn to manage their energy and focus, positive changes can become rather dramatic. If an organization could actually become 100% forward-focused, the Net Forward Energy Ratio would be 100 divided by 0. That equals infinity and,

Think of a time recently when the energy level dropped in your organization. What caused it to happen?

How was the organization impacted?

theoretically, such an organization could accomplish anything.

However, reaching a Net Forward Energy Ratio of infinity is not what this discussion is about. It is about continually renewing, continually moving closer and closer to where we ultimately want to be. As we have seen, even small changes in forward focus are extremely impactive.

As the Net Forward Energy Ratio is enhanced, people begin looking more at what is right about their work environment than at what is wrong about it. They become more open to possibilities and begin building on what is working and on what they want more of. They become excited about what they are doing. Their self-confidence rises.

One of the critical, strategic roles of enlightened, renewing leaders is to focus the energy of their organizations. Many influences every day already manage, guide, change, and direct the energy of our people. Leaders can manage the organization's Net Forward Energy Ratio by consciously making the choice of where to focus their energy and their people's energy. There may be no better way a leader can leverage his or her time than through empowering people by helping them maintain their optimal focus.

The concepts surrounding the Net Forward Energy Ratio are not to be confused with classical motivation. Motivation efforts often try to bring in outside energy and add it to the system. At its best, motivation is a quick fix or a Band-Aid supplied by someone else. At its worst, traditional motivation only addresses the symptom—low energy—without resolving the underlying issue—what causes the energy to be low.

The approach we have been discussing focuses and aligns the energy that is already in an organization. This existing energy is virtually inexhaustible. Remember the light bulb/laser beam illustration? The energy is already present. The key centers on accessing and focusing that energy.

NAMING OUR MODEL OF CHOICES

During the course of this book, we have been using a model to provide a simple illustration of the choices we have for how we focus our attention and energy. For example, as a reminder of the choices we have about whether to focus on the reasons we cannot accomplish an objective or on the results we want to achieve, we might use the graphic model shown below.

The name we give this model of the choices we have, or the focus model, is NeFER® (pronounced like never, but with an F sound), which comes from Net Forward Energy Ratio. We would call this particular example the reasons-results NeFER. NeFERs suggest that we have a choice of where to focus our attention and energy. We can focus either on the reasons we cannot accomplish the objective or on the results we desire. In this case, "reasons" is *back-*

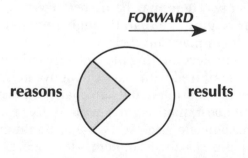

ward on the NeFER and "results" is *forward* on the NeFER. If we focus backward on the NeFER, we hold ourselves back. If we focus forward on the NeFER, we move forward toward our goal.

FRAMEWORK FOR CONTINUOUS RENEWAL

With the help of numerous clients, we have developed a structured approach to managing the focus and energy of individuals and teams in ways that create the paradigm shift in mindsets we are looking for. While any focus mechanism or approach that is directed to the forward side of an appropriate NeFER supports the mindset shift over time, we have found this five-step framework to be particularly effective.

It represents a series of focus choices, and it can be extremely effective for problem-solving, vision or mission development, performance appraisals, project and performance reviews, customer service planning, and many other day-to-day tactical business needs. It is so versatile that the same generic framework, which we call the Framework for Continuous Renewal, also can accurately be called a Framework for Continuous Improvement, a Framework for Total Quality Consciousness®, a Framework for Effective Problem-Solving, a Framework for Continuous Quality Improvement, a Framework for Creating Paradigm Shifts, a Framework for Leadership, etc.

Framework for Continuous Renewal

1. Celebrate the small successes you are achieving.

2. Research extensively what you are doing to generate these successes.

3. Continually reclarify (refocus on) in great detail your specific objective(s).

4. Help all parties (customers, shareholders, the organization, team, each person) understand the benefits of achieving the objectives.

5. Continually search for what you could be doing more of, better or differently, to move closer to the objectives.

Reviewing the five steps more closely, what do you notice about them that would support the desired mindset shift?

What is it about this particular combination of focus statements that is especially effective?

How do they support dealing with problems in an empowering way?

What is the overall intention behind this framework?

Let's look more closely at how the five steps of the Framework for Continuous Renewal work. Remember, these are generic elements of a five-step process. The specific "words" may be different depending on how the process is being used. The *intention* of the framework is more important than the specific words.

Notice how Step 1 focuses clearly on the forward side of the focus model, the "what's-working" side of the NeFER instead of the "what's-not-working" side. As we have discussed, this energizes people and gets them communicating in a positive way. The more people are energized by looking at the positive side of an issue the more their minds are open to the possibilities.

Step 2 analyzes the reasons *why* what you are doing is working and is effective. This is far more energizing and enjoyable than the more typical approach of analyzing what is *not* working. In addition, Step 2 supports understanding the real causes of effectiveness. This clear understanding allows people to repeat consciously what works more frequently, including utilizing it in other areas. This is the learning step.

The combination of Steps 1 and 2 is extremely empowering. By the time a team has completed these two steps, energy and creativity are high and communication is open. It has them feeling good about what they are doing, and their self-esteem is enhanced. These are nurturing, encouraging steps. The team is functioning from an effective state of mind that is necessary for moving forward toward solutions or desired outcomes.

With this high level of positive energy now available, we are ready to move on to Step 3. This step clarifies as specifically as possible the end objective. It describes as completely as possible what it will be like when the team achieves its goal. The objective here is to create a crystal-clear vision of the desired result. To the extent the objective is clear, it will pull the team toward creating it.

So far, Steps 1 and 2 have provided the energy and empowered state of mind necessary to deal effectively with an issue or bring about a desired result. Then, Step 3 created a detailed description of the desired outcome or result. Notice a gap has been created between Step 1 and Step 3.

The gap, or void, is the difference between what is already working and where you ultimately want to be. This gap acts like a vacuum, pulling in the resources needed to fill it. It naturally energizes the individual or team to want to close the gap. The gap represents what needs to be done to meet the objective.

In the old paradigm, we would meet to discuss a problem and get mired in all the reasons why we had this problem and all the reasons we couldn't resolve it. Energy often drops like a rock in these "problem-solving" sessions. So much energy goes into defending ourselves that little energy or creativity is left over for finding solutions.

For comparative purposes, let's call this new approach Framework for Effective Problem-Solving. Using this framework, we effectively deal with the problem without getting mired in it. We simply generate energy and creativity, get clear on the outcome we want, then see what it takes to fill the gap. The situation is not seen as a problem but as an opportunity to move from where we are toward where we want to be. It is truly a solution orientation.

Step 4 supports the team members in getting clear about what achieving the objectives will do for all parties concerned. By focusing on the higher levels of value first (i.e., benefits for customers, the organization, and the team), it becomes much easier then to home in on what achieving the objectives would do for each participant personally. This is the "what's in it for me" piece. Once people are clear about the personal benefit of achieving an objective, they are motivated to do what needs to be done to make it happen. They have bought in to the objective and are committed to meeting the goal.

Note that the "what's in it for me" will vary widely from person to person. The benefit for one individual might be directly personal, while another's benefit might be just feeling part of a successful team. What the benefit is, is not important, only that the individuals are clear about it for themselves.

This approach generates a high level of energy and creativity, as well as creating an effective mindset. It clarifies the objective in great detail, and each person becomes clear about the personal value in achieving that objective. All that remains is to use the creativity, energy, and commitment of the team to determine what actions they need to take to move closer to achieving the objective.

Accomplishing Steps 1 through 4 prepares us for Step 5. Once we have generated the energy, creativity, and clarity of our objective in the previous steps, the final step is simpler and more enjoyable. Because of the attitude with which people come into this step, the solutions are usually clear and often obvious.

The communication officers in the Denver Communications Center of the Colorado State Patrol were receiving an average of about six complaints a week from their own people. The people didn't like each other, had a high sick-leave rate, and constantly bickered and gossiped; rumors were the norm rather than the exception. Teaching new skills and techniques did not improve the situation.

Major Don Lamb describes it this way, "A positive self-image is very, very critical. I'm finding that in most teams, the number one factor is trust. That's the big word that's always coming up in all of the meetings that I have been conducting. One of the big things that occurs is that when the trust level goes down, communications start shutting off and positive self-image really starts to drop. People start focusing on the negative rather than the positive, and the more they focus on the negative, the more their self-image goes down. It's like a vicious spiral and a whirlpool that takes people down, that takes whole teams down, that takes whole companies down."

By consistently using the Framework for Continuous Renewal as a basis for their meetings, the communication officers created a dramatic shift in their people's attitudes. Complaints were reduced from six a week to one a month.

"That's a tremendous drop," states Major Lamb. "Sick

leave has also been reduced dramatically simply by addressing attitudes directly. Those people work so well together now it is amazing. Those are the kind of measurable
results that mean something to me. The more we use these
approaches with the right intent, the more trusting our
people become. The more we trust our people, the more
they begin to trust us, trust themselves, and trust each
other."

> More information as to how the morale was
> transformed at the Colorado State Patrol is
> available in a two-page article. For a com-
> plimentary copy of "Quality: The Human
> Factor," call 1-800-798-9881.

> *What has been most frustrating for you about
> more traditional approaches to issue reso-
> lution? What level of true success have they
> achieved in your organization?*
>
> *What level of commitment to the solutions
> have they generated?*
>
> *In what ways has the level of commitment
> affected the team's ability to achieve desired
> results?*
>
> *What benefits would your team enjoy from
> having a higher level of commitment and
> ownership?*

Two aspects of our focus are very important. First, it is
critically important to nurture and grow our organization's

most important assets and resources—our people. If we spend all of our time and energy nurturing, however, there will be no time left over for creating results. Therefore, our second critical focus is on the objectives we want to achieve and how we are going to accomplish them. This sets the expectations for the outcomes we need.

It is vitally important to balance the energy focused on these two factors: supporting our people and creating results. Notice how the "Framework for Continuous Renewal" provides that balance. Steps 1 and 2 provide the encouragement and growth of our people. Steps 3, 4, and 5 focus on creating results. Both factors are essential to long-term success.

As discussed, managing energy involves consciously choosing how we focus the energy we already have. Focusing our attention as much as possible on the forward side of an appropriate focus model, or NeFER, is critical to the ongoing renewal of our people and organization.

Change-Friendly Highlights

1. In every stage of life, we bring our attitudes and our personal collection of paradigms, which form the basis for our actions and our opinions.

2. To establish a renewing organization, the primary need is to bring about a fundamental paradigm shift in the way people think, behave, and manage. The shift is from being change-resistant to change-friendly.

3. When enough people within an organization become change-friendly, renewal is naturally continuous.

4. The ability of an organization to move forward depends upon how much productive energy people are expending while moving toward the organization's objectives. This is the Net Forward Energy Ratio.

5. It is vitally important to balance the energy focused on two key factors:
   (a) Nurturing and growth of the organization's most important assets and resources—its people.
   (b) What needs to be achieved—the organizational objectives.

You are searching for the magic key that will unlock the door to the source of power; and yet you have the key in your own hands, and you may use it the moment you learn to control your thoughts.

NAPOLEON HILL
Think and Grow Rich

7

ASKING VERSUS TELLING

Tell me and I'll forget; show me and I may remember; involve me and I'll understand.

Chinese Proverb

Do It My Way

Think about what happens most often when we decide
to make a major change in the way our organization does
things. Typically we call everyone together, *tell* them the
new idea, and give them all *our* good reasons as to why it
is important to do things the new way. At best, we attempt
to sell the change by presenting all the benefits *we* think
it will produce. This part of the change process does not
take very long and is reasonably effortless.

The next part, acceptance, or buy-in, and successful implementation can seemingly take forever, if, in fact, it ever
occurs. Later, when analyzing the change efforts, we con-
clude that, at best, there was something wrong with the
way we presented the idea that caused a lack of acceptance
by the people and poor results. At worst, we may feel that
our employees were just obstinate. Both may be true—but
for a reason so simple it generally is not even recognized.

> *How do you feel when someone tells you how
> it's going to be, giving you no choice or input
> in the matter?*   angry / unimportant
>
> *What might our people be hearing when we
> tell them our good ideas?*   I'm great / smart
>   you're not

People tend to resist changes that are thrust upon them,
while they naturally support ideas and changes they help
create. "Telling," by its very nature, lays the foundation for
defensiveness and resistance, because it thrusts change
upon others. This is especially true when the telling involves
notifying people how they personally need to change.

The reason for this is simple: When we tell someone
what to do differently and why it is important to do it, we
convey subtle—even if unintended—messages along with
the basic information. These may suggest, "My way is better

than yours" or "Your way is wrong." Whether or not a negative message is implied or intended, often the receivers of the message may still hear or feel negativity and become hurt or offended—a common response to criticism. In business, as in other areas of life, resistance often follows this response. Resistance is energy spent on not doing something, on avoiding change itself, or on fearing a change. It is a defensive reaction, a natural, self-protective response. This resistance may show up as complacency, lack of commitment, nonaction, outward opposition, or subtle sabotage.

Ed Tilford, former director of software engineering for a major computer firm, provided us with an example. His team of software engineers clearly needed a software program to help them perform structural analysis. After researching the available solutions himself, Ed chose a package that he felt met the team's needs and bought it.

Though the $200,000 software package addressed the structural analysis problems they were experiencing, his team exhibited substantial resistance to using the software. They finally did acquiesce; however, they certainly did not buy in, and this was obvious from their lack of commitment to using the program. After a long period of dealing with the team's resistance, Ed held a meeting with his software engineers. The bottom line was simply that they just didn't like the software he had purchased.

Ed then turned the problem over to his team to handle themselves. After some investigation, they chose another program. They were very happy with their choice and used it enthusiastically to advance the work they were doing. Curiously, Ed found that the program they chose was extremely similar to the one that he had originally selected. In fact, it had been developed by a team that had left the company that made the original program. The primary difference between the two programs was that the team got behind the one they had chosen.

It is important to note, though, that people don't resist change as much as they resist being changed. As we discussed in Chapter 4, when we come up with our own ideas for change we are not likely to resist them, but watch us automatically have some degree of resistance to someone else's ideas no matter how good or logical they are.

Our degree of resistance is likely to be inversely proportional to our level of self-esteem. Indeed, the essence of resistance to change revolves around people's self-image, or how they feel about themselves. Reactive Thinkers suffer from low self-esteem, and thus will have high resistance to change. The higher self-esteem of the Creative Thinker results in less resistance to change. Creative Thinkers are not as threatened by change.

Think of a time when you had a good idea and couldn't wait to tell someone. When you did tell them, what was their level of enthusiasm compared to yours?

Did you find yourself trying to convince them how good the idea was?

How did you feel about their response?

WHOSE PERSPECTIVE COUNTS, ANYWAY?

Traditionally, management has responded to resistance to change by trying to convince people of the importance of achieving an objective. In many cases, these leaders can't understand why their people are resistant at all. This is, in part, because most people in leadership roles don't tend to see the world the way a Reactive Thinker does. Their tendency to be more like the Creative Thinker separates them from the rest of the pack and is often a factor helping them rise to roles of leadership. At the same time, this different perspective makes it difficult for them to understand the behavior of the more Reactive Thinkers, making up 80% or more of their people.

Like most of us, these leaders sometimes forget or find it difficult to look at the world from a perspective other than their own. They forget that many other people see the world through a set of eyes conditioned to focus on what's wrong. These Reactive Thinkers tend to look at any idea or change for how it might hurt them instead of for the opportunity it might provide.

Yet, we only see what is important from our own perspective. And what is important to us may not be to someone else. Even if we really try to see a situation from another's perspective—to put ourselves in their shoes, so to speak—the conclusions we come up with still represent only *our* perspective of what they think.

These differences in perspectives create major problems when using the telling approach to change implementation. They can sabotage even the best-intentioned telling actions. For example, a plant manager for a large manufacturing firm noticed he was getting many complaints from production line assemblers about huge gaps in the flow of units and parts to their division. Assemblers were having to wait for work to do, and, since they were on a piece-rate pay plan, it was costing them dearly.

In an effort to solve the problem, the plant manager called in a traditional consulting firm to study the situation. The consultants said they needed to be able to track the production flow through each stage and determine where and how the snags were developing. They recommended installing electronic sensing devices and video cameras at key points along the line.

On the day the instruments were to be installed, the manager called his assemblers together. He explained that he had heard their complaints, that the company was spending nearly $20,000 to find the snags, and that management would spend whatever it took to correct the problem. He ended his speech by reaffirming how much the company valued its employees and wanted to do its part to enable them to make as much money as possible. He was taken aback by the subdued response he received.

As promised, the instruments were all installed and turned on. Within a week, however, more than half of the devices had been sabotaged by grease guns and electric staplers. A couple of camera lenses had even been broken with hammers.

"Why?" he asked angrily in a subsequent meeting with the employees. "We were trying to solve *your* problems!"

After a long, tense silence, someone answered, "We don't appreciate 'Big Brother' spying on us!"

"That was not our intent at all," the plant manager countered.

"Look, we're not stupid," the brave one replied. "We all know it's just a matter of time before you put the finger on slower workers and fire them."

The equipment was quickly removed, and the solution stalled indefinitely.

The plant manager's intentions were good. He even recognized the importance of keeping people informed about his actions. But he *told* them how he was going to solve their problem. That approach cost the company a lot of money. Even worse, it damaged the manager's credibility with the very people he was trying to help.

---

*W*hat resistance have you faced recently to what you considered to be a superb idea? *Focus*

*W*hat insights have you gained from this book so far that are most helpful in understanding what caused the resistance? *Bottom-up*

*I*n thinking back about the situation, how might the way the idea was presented have contributed to the resistance? *Big line*

*W*hat would you do differently next time? *Slow roll out*

A DIFFERENT APPROACH

What would have happened if the plant manager had asked the assemblers to participate in finding a solution? Our experience in similar situations suggests that they might very well have suggested using cameras and sensing devices themselves, come up with a modified approach to solving the problem or found a less costly and/or more effective solution.

In any case, the assemblers would have supported whatever solution was implemented because it was *their solution*. By devising it themselves, they would have felt they possessed ownership of it and would consequently buy-in to its implementation. Rather than resisting the change, they would welcome it and help it happen successfully. Indeed, they would have a personal stake in that success.

Let's look at how to approach a similar situation in a different manner. The management team of an east coast manufacturing firm with a long-standing adversarial relationship with its union found itself confronted with yet another grievance. In the past, management had always responded to complaints by *telling* the union how it was willing to resolve the situation. The union would then typically *tell* management what it wanted. This counterproposal would then lead to a focus on the differences between the two, and conflict lines inevitably were drawn.

This time, however, the management team decided to handle the grievance differently. The members discussed the problem and came to some conclusions about what a satisfactory outcome would look like from their perspective. During the following week the operations manager casually *asked* different members of the union's executive committee for their ideas about ways to best resolve the grievance.

Within 10 days the union president presented the management team with a proposal. This proposed resolution was surprisingly close to what management had already decided would work for them. The grievance was resolved much more quickly and with less tension and conflict than in the past. These results were achieved by management *asking* the union members what they thought it would take to resolve the grievance rather than *telling* them the way it was going to be handled.

In your leadership role, what was the last significant change you implemented or tried to implement?

How did your individual people respond outwardly to the plan?

How did they respond in implementing the change?

How did the response vary among your people?

How effective was the change?

What did you do that best contributed to its success?

THE MANAGER-EMPLOYEE REALITY GAP

Taken in part from a study by the U.S. Chamber of Commerce (*The Balanced Program,* ©1986), this information illustrates the gap that can exist when leaders don't *ask* what's important to their people. It represents a ranking by order of importance of what employees want versus what managers think they want:

What is important to employees?

Perspective of:

Items ranked by employees and employers in order of importance from 1 to 10 (1 highest):	Employee	Employer
(1) Appreciation	1	8
(2) Feeling in on things	2	10
(3) Help on personal problems	3	9

This gap between what *really* is important to workers and what management *thinks* is important gives us a strong hint about what needs to happen to implement successful change and develop a renewing organization. How could we possibly expect to get the best from our people unless they are getting what they most want from us? How can we give them what they want if we don't know what that is? The simple answer is to ask rather than second-guess our people's needs.

Notice that the three items most important to employees are soft issues. When employees feel misunderstood by corporate leaders and when they don't get what they want from them, employee morale drops. As the attitude shifts downward, so does energy and focus. Performance follows the downward trend as productivity, quality, customer service, and other hard measures fall as well. Furthermore, this situation breeds destructive relationships between employees and management, which further incites the downward spiral of disappointment, morale, attitudes, energy, focus, performance, and relationships.

Just how much discretionary effort/energy is being held back that could be available to apply toward increasing productivity, enhancing customer service, cutting costs, or improving quality? Daniel Yankelovich's study shows that: "About a fifth of the workers feel they're giving everything they can to the job; another fifth don't want to give anything more than the little they are now giving; but the 60% in the middle say they would give more to their work if there were more in it for them. . . ."

> **What would it mean to your organization if 60% of the people gave just 10% more to their jobs?**

A typical response from management to the statement that 60% "would give more to their work if there were more in it for them" is that the workers are talking about more money—a hard issue. Yet, virtually every study and all our combined years of experience show money has much less importance to employees than being appreciated and feeling in on things and participating in what is going on within the organization.

When we work with teams and ask them to clarify what they want and need more of from leadership to enable them to do a better job, money is seldom, if ever, mentioned. In those rare instances where money is brought up, it takes little probing to get to what people are really saying. The issue is almost always "they're going to have to pay me more money if I'm going to have to put up with this B.S." The "B.S." is being unappreciated and excluded, which are by-products of not being asked.

THE REAL EXPERTS

The *real experts* about an organization—the people with the solutions to resolve practically every issue an organization faces—are *its own people*. Rather than seeking out consultants from the outside for expert advice, the real challenge lies in learning to access the untapped wealth of expertise and knowledge found within the organization it- self. As Wolf Schmitt, president and chief operating officer of Rubbermaid, emphasized in a speech at that company's annual shareholder's meeting in 1991, ". . . everyone is an expert in a highly specialized field . . . his or her own job. Odds are, each individual knows better than anyone how to improve it. . . ."

By *asking* questions leaders help their people *discover for themselves* what is important for them in doing what is necessary for the company. This discovery process improves their self-confidence and self-esteem, empowering them in the process. Concurrently, they take ownership of the so- lution, because they have participated in developing it.

> *What has been the value of the questions we have asked you, as the reader, in this book so far?*

There is at least one additional benefit of asking instead of telling. When we ask, we put out subtle messages that are important for building the self-esteem and self-confi- dence of our people, which is the key to shifting their think- ing paradigm. The messages are, "I care about what you think," and, "Your opinion is important, and it counts around here." These are important acknowledgments for the people in any organization. The more people feel that they make a difference, the better they will feel about what they are doing. The better they feel about what they are doing, the more their self-esteem is enhanced and the more contribution they will make.

One of the least productive aspects of making bricks at a nationally prominent Denver-based firm was the equip- ment changeover, or setup, from producing one style of brick to another. Management had spent countless hours in meetings trying to find a way to accomplish the productivity-killing task in less time. No matter what they tried the result was pretty much the same—two hours to make the change.

After helping their management team go through a paradigm shift in their approach from telling to asking, they brought their people together to discuss the issue. The basic theme was, "If there were no limitations on what you could do, what would you do to complete the equipment setup better and more quickly?" As a result of the ideas from that one meeting, the changeover time was reduced to under 30 minutes. The people had the answers all along. They just had not been asked or listened to.

The people on any team possess tremendous knowledge, wisdom, creativity, and energy. Enlightened leaders access this wealth of experience and empower their people through the effective use of questions.

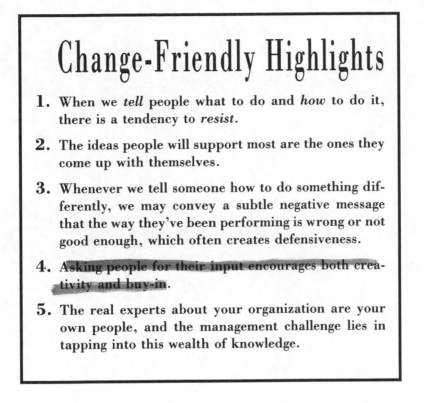

Change-Friendly Highlights

1. When we *tell* people what to do and *how* to do it, there is a tendency to *resist*.

2. The ideas people will support most are the ones they come up with themselves.

3. Whenever we tell someone how to do something differently, we may convey a subtle negative message that the way they've been performing is wrong or not good enough, which often creates defensiveness.

4. Asking people for their input encourages both creativity and buy-in.

5. The real experts about your organization are your own people, and the management challenge lies in tapping into this wealth of knowledge.

By examining and understanding the past, we can move into the future unencumbered by it. We become free to express ourselves, rather than endlessly trying to prove ourselves.

WARREN BENNIS
On Becoming a Leader

8

THE ULTIMATE EMPOWERMENT TOOL

The teacher, if indeed wise, does not bid you to enter the house of their wisdom, but leads you to the threshold of your own mind.

KAHLIL GIBRAN
Lebanese Poet and Painter (1883–1931)

COMBINING FORWARD FOCUS AND QUESTIONS

In previous chapters we have looked at focus as the primary way of creating a paradigm shift in the mindset of our people, at the NeFER as a model of the choices we have about where to focus our attention and energy, and at asking as a tool for empowerment. With all these concepts, our goal is to move people from the disempowered state of Reactive Thinking to the empowered state of Creative Thinking. This represents a paradigm shift in how we focus our attention and energy.

Each of these tools is powerful in its own right, but there is another tool that takes empowerment and effectiveness to a far higher level—much higher than any of these separate concepts. We call this tool Effective Questions (EQs). It combines the power of focusing on the forward side of the NeFER with the power of asking questions. This combination creates much greater results than the sum of the results achieved by either of the individual tools.

Yes, it is that simple. There exists a certain way of asking questions so empowering that clients have labeled them "The Ultimate Empowerment Tool." Those leaders who master the simple art of asking EQs and listening, unleash the energy and creativity of their people and focus it like a laser on what needs to be done to continually improve their organizations and fulfill the people working within them.

The better we become at asking EQs, as well as effectively listening, the more consistently we and our people can accomplish mutually satisfying objectives. This approach to seeking solutions separates Enlightened Leaders from managers who are continuously plagued by personnel and resistance problems. Indeed, by asking EQs we empower our employees, thus creating a willingness on their part to pursue change, solutions or objectives with minimal, if any, resistance.

WHAT MAKES EFFECTIVE QUESTIONS EFFECTIVE?

In simple terms, the human mind, which is far more powerful than any computer devised by mankind, basically works by continually looking for answers to questions it receives from a variety of sources. No matter what questions are asked, answers *are* generated at some point. Just as a car runs differently depending upon what type of fuel it uses, the mind runs differently depending upon the kind of questions it is asked to answer. For this reason, we must look at the questions with which we fuel our minds. What kind of questions are we running on?

The Reactive Thinking 80%rs runs on questions like, "What's wrong with this situation?" "How is this going to hurt me?" "How can I avoid being blamed for this?" and "Why does this always happen to me?" Notice that the answers to these questions, which the mind works hard to provide, do not support moving forward in life. Instead, they tend to keep us trapped right where we are, perpetuating our situation rather than looking for alternatives to that situation. As we have seen, questions like these tend to de-energize and disempower us and make us defensive and generally nonproductive.

The Creative Thinking 20%ers, on the other hand, tend to run on questions like, "What value can we gain from this situation?" "How can we benefit from this?" "How can we turn this into an opportunity?" and "What can we do to make this a win for everyone?" As we have seen, questions such as these empower and give us information we can use to move forward in life. In this scenario, therefore, our minds are continually focused on generating forward-moving ideas and solutions. If we then act on these ideas, we move forward, and the results produced from that action empower us to even greater levels.

By utilizing EQs, we consciously choose the kinds of questions that fuel our mind and guide us. We choose the questions that will be most supportive of our continuing growth and success, thus interrupting the naturally destructive mindset of Reactive Thinking and forcing ourselves to think more creatively and effectively. If we consistently provide ourselves—and others—with EQs as a discipline, we will soon become reconditioned in the way we think. In other words, the desired paradigm shift occurs when this new Creative Thinking mode is internalized and becomes automatic. While the effect of this shift is a powerful one for individuals, imagine the synergy of an entire team or organization on EQs provided by leadership.

When Steve Knox was promoted to district director of the U.S. Customs Service's Philadelphia office, one of the first things he did was to call his new staff together for a meeting.

Anyone who has ever been in the position of getting a new boss can probably relate to how Steve's people felt going into this meeting. Everyone figured he was going to do the reactive "I'm the new boss, here's what I see is wrong, and here's how we are going to start doing things differently" bit. So, the people came in to the meeting apprehensive and prepared to defend themselves with files, charts, "reasons," and excuses.

Instead, Steve used EQs. He asked each manager to share with him and the others the two or three things working the best in their department. Then he asked what they would like to do differently to improve their areas, and how each change would create the desired result. The team was incredibly energized by this approach and subsequently has grown from this foundation into a very effective team.

BENEFITS OF ASKING EFFECTIVE QUESTIONS

EQs provide a vital empowerment bridge from the mindset we currently have to the mindset we want to possess.

They accomplish this by effectively addressing mindset issues in a number of different ways:

- **EQs get people to think.**

- **EQs empower people by allowing them to discover their own answers, thus developing self-responsibility and transference of ownership for the results.**

- **EQs "mine" the real experts, your people, for their "gold"—better ways to achieve the objectives.**

- **EQs create Total Quality Consciousness (TQC) throughout an organization.**

- **EQs help people realize, on an ongoing basis, how what they are doing contributes to the whole (the overall objective, the mission or vision).**

- **EQs develop people who feel fulfilled, satisfied, and valued.**

- **EQs build positive attitudes and self-esteem in individual members of a team.**

- **EQs remove blocks and open people up to unexplored possibilities while inviting discovery, creativity, and innovation.**

- **EQs unlock the untapped potential of an organization by accessing people's "discretionary work effort."**

- **EQs help us determine what it will take to do what has not been done before.**

- **EQs guide us toward where we want to go while providing value out of where we have been.**

- **EQs enable leaders to understand what a person**

or team wants and the conditions upon which they will buy in to organizational goals.

- EQs involve people in management and decision-making processes, thus generating commitment to the solution or answer.

- EQs develop alignment within teams and draw out the optimum performance from individual members and the team as a whole.

- EQs generate alignment with a shared vision or desired outcome.

- EQs create a high-energy, high-trust environment.

- EQs encourage people to identify, clarify, and express their wants or needs.

- EQs encourage people to take risks.

- EQs recondition people from only knowing *what* to think to knowing *how* to think.

- EQs connect the *what's in it for me* with what needs to be done.

- EQs nurture deep relationships.

- EQs dissolve resistance to change.

QUESTIONS THAT DISEMPOWER/EMPOWER

Questions can be productive, or they can be counterproductive. They can energize us or drain our energy. They can bring out creativity or squelch it. Questions can open us up and build trust, or they can cause defensiveness. Sometimes we meet someone who asks great questions that we feel eager to answer and that make us feel *empowered*. Occasionally, we meet someone who asks a lot of questions that somehow make us feel put on the spot, intimidated, and *disempowered.*

To clarify the difference between an EQ and a question that is less effective or even detrimental to our objectives, let's utilize a now familiar NeFER.

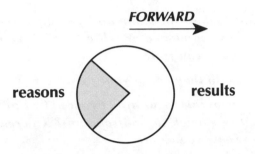

As we've said before, we have a choice of focusing our attention and energy on the results we want to accomplish or on all the reasons we cannot achieve them. When the focus is one the reasons, we are probably in a defensive or reactive mode and working to assure that we are not blamed for the problems. This disempowering mode drains our energy.

Let's look at some questions to which we can probably all relate. Please read them thoroughly, and try to remember a time when you might have heard similar ones:

"Why are you behind schedule?"

"What's the problem on this project?"

"Why are you so far behind the other team?"

"What's your problem?"

"Who isn't keeping up?"

"Who did that?"

"Why did you do that?"

"Who made that decision?"

"Don't you know better than that?"

"Who wants to tell the boss about this?"

What do these questions do for your personal sense of confidence or self-esteem? How do they make you feel?

Where do they cause your focus to be?

How does this focus affect your ability to be creative enough to find solutions? To create the results you want?

If you were bombarded consistently by these kinds of questions, how would it impact your energy level? How would it affect your attitudes about your work? How would it likely affect your long-term performance and satisfaction?

On which side of the NeFER do these questions focus?

You may remember unpleasant times when you have heard these questions, times when the focus was on the back side of the NeFER. You might even remember the feelings you had when the questions were being asked. Thinking about the situation, you might remember being somewhat defensive, low on energy (except possibly the energy of anger) and definitely not focused on what needed to be done to resolve the issues. Many of us might find these questions to be somewhat threatening, especially if our confidence was a little lacking at that moment, and our attitude and creativity were not at their best. The situation might have left us feeling discouraged.

If after reading the questions you did not relate to any

of the feelings or reactions described in the last paragraph, you probably fall into that upper 2%, the Creative Thinkers who are so personally empowered that they cannot even imagine people having problems with such questions. If you fall into this category, we suggest you use EQs to discover how other people relate to the previous set of questions; it could be enlightening.

Now, let's look at some different questions. Please read them slowly and thoughtfully, allowing yourself to be aware of how they affect you:

> "How do you feel about the project so far?"

> "What have you accomplished so far that you are most pleased with?"

> "What about that accomplishment do you most appreciate?"

> "What else?"

> "How would you describe the way you want this project to turn out?"

> "What are your specific objectives?"

> "Which of those objectives do you think will be easiest to accomplish?"

> "Which will be most difficult?"

> "What will be the benefits for our customers if you can meet all these objectives? For our company? For our team? For you personally?"

> "What key things need to happen to achieve the objective?"

> "What kind of support do you need to assure success?"

Notice how this second set of questions is in alignment with the Framework for Continuous Improvement in Chap-

> *W*hat do these questions do for your personal sense of confidence or self-esteem? How do they make you feel?
>
> *H*ow does this focus affect your ability to be creative enough to find solutions? To create the results you want?
>
> *I*f you were consistently asked these kinds of questions, how would it impact your energy level? How would it affect your attitude about work? How would it likely affect your long-term performance and satisfaction?
>
> *O*n which side of the NeFER do these questions focus?
>
> *I*n terms of impact on you personally, what is the difference between the two sets of questions?
>
> *H*ow would the two sets of questions impact your people differently?

ter 6. They tend to be focused on either what is already working, which is energizing and supportive, or on clarifying the objectives, which creates a clear target or goal. They may also focus on benefits, which is why we want to achieve the objective, or on what needs to be done to move toward the objective, which is the action plan. All these questions yield responses that support moving forward toward the objectives. By adding the *asking* element, people get the additional benefit of discovering the answers for themselves. This generates automatic buy-in and commitment to the solutions they find.

Whether people become part of the problem or the solution relates directly to the way leaders ask questions. If we focus on the back side of the NeFER—the "Reasons," "What's not working?" and "What's wrong?"—the questions threaten self-esteem, and people tend to get mired in the problems. In this defensive mode people are more likely to see themselves as part of the problem rather than the source of solutions. If we spotlight the "Results," "What's working?" "What's right?" and "What do we want more of?" side of the NeFER, the questions are encouraging and we point team members toward results and solutions. Since we get what we focus upon, we move closer and closer to our objectives, and people become part of the solution.

FUNDAMENTALS OF EFFECTIVE QUESTIONS

What makes one question more effective than another lies in its essence, and that essence cannt be defined by a set of guidelines that we can follow. They are more a function of where people are *coming from* in asking them than in what is said. Yet, we can describe some of the most common characteristics of EQs.

• EQS ARE OPEN-ENDED.

Our people are the real experts about our organizations and what needs to be done in them. They have the solutions; we just need a way to access these solutions. We can do so by encouraging the normally lazy human mind to *think* and our people to *express* their thoughts and ideas.

Questions that call for a "yes" or "no" answer, called closed-ended questions, tend to discourage people from thinking and talking and encourage them to give only limited information. Worse, they limit the possible choice of answers to two. And these two answers are basically judgments. When asked to make a judgment about something, we usually close up, rather than open up, for fear of having our answer judged in return.

Notice the contrast between questions like, "Do you like your job?" or "Is the project going well?" and questions like, "What do you like about your job?" "What aspects of the project are going well?" or "What aspects need additional work?"

What do you think the differences are in these two sets of questions?

Which ones cause more thinking?

Which ones are more energizing?

From which set of questions are the answers likely to be more informative?

The second set of questions are open-ended. Open-ended questions give people the opportunity to search deeply within themselves for possibilities rather than making "yes" or "no" judgments. These questions encourage people to think and express themselves and to explain how they feel, what they want or what they think. They also invite creativity and empowerment.

• EQs FOCUS ON THE FORWARD SIDE OF THE NeFER.

EQs generally focus on the objective of increasing the amount of energy and attention directed to where we want to go and to what we want more of. An organization's Net Forward Energy Ratio will increase dramatically, as well as naturally, as more and more people become masters at the art of asking EQs. So, to positively direct the energy of our people, we focus on "What do we need to do to get to where we want to be?" rather than on "What's wrong with where we are?"

---

*R*eview the two different sets of questions offered on pages 143 and 145. In what ways do they differ in terms of which side of the NeFER they focus on?

*W*hat differences are there in impact on attitude, energy, feelings, and performance between the two focuses?

*W*hich one is more effective?

• EQs ASK "WHAT" OR "HOW" INSTEAD OF "WHY."

"Why" questions, though they often appear to get to the heart of the matter, seem to generate instant resistance and defensiveness. Most of us have painful memories of times when people used "why" questions to build a case against us. There seems to be a natural reaction to these questions, feeling that someone asking us a "why" question is challenging what we did, trying to make us wrong. We feel we have to justify what we did. We might naturally become defensive and shut down. When we shut down, the creativity needed to move forward with solutions is lost.

A "what" or "how" question generally encourages openness and lowers resistance. Also, questions that begin with "what" will usually encourage multiple responses. To find the best solutions, a series of "what" or "how" questions can prove invaluable. Keep asking, "What else?" until it is uncomfortable to do so. Then, do it one more time. Often, the real gems come late in the process as a person's thinking goes deeper and deeper.

"How" questions will generate similar responses as "what" questions. "How" questions usually elicit only single responses; however, when you follow up with multiple "What-else?" questions, you will receive multiple answers.

If the questions being asked are of a "What's-wrong?" variety, we tend to close down and become defensive. The only way to answer them is to own up to being part of the problem. When the questions are of the "What's-working-now?" and "What-do-we-want-to-do?" type, formulating an answer supports progress toward a solution. Then we feel a part of the solution and safe enough to open up and offer our ideas.

> *N*otice the difference in the "*why*" and "*what*" questions asked earlier in this chapter on pages 143 and 145. What is the difference in impact on attitude, energy, feelings, and performance between the two focuses?
>
> *W*hich are more effective and how?

Note: It is essential for leaders to develop an awareness of when a question has generated defensiveness so they can step back and rephrase it.

• EQs HELP PEOPLE LEARN THROUGH THE PROCESS OF ANSWERING.

In many circumstances, Enlightened Leaders ask EQs not only so that *they* can hear the answers given to them but so *the persons asked* can hear *their own* answers and, thereby, gain clarity for themselves or internalize something they have grasped only intellectually.

Indeed, the answers that are most effective for people are their own. When people are told answers, they may understand them intellectually, but they will still need to clarify and internalize them for themselves. Our natural resistance to someone else's answers or ways of doing things—no matter how good or logical they may be—may prevent us from ever internalizing them. The internalization happens much faster when people's answers originate from themselves.

An example of the power of questions has to do with a major insurance company whose management team noticed that the average salesperson's sales dropped off dramatically after 18 months regardless of the training received.* They did intensive research to uncover what caused this phenomenon. Numerous ideas were suggested about the reasons for this consistent decrease in sales, including one that always gets a good laugh—"Maybe it's because they ran out of relatives and friends."

The results of the research provided far more interesting information, however. During the early months after training, the salespeople would stick closely to the company's recommended approach of asking prospective customers many thought-provoking questions and carefully listening to their answers. They would typically spend 45 minutes or an hour on this process. In fact, they became better and better at asking EQs that generated much thought and discussion by the client. This questioning process was also very supportive of the client getting clear about their future financial needs.

Right around 18 months in their development, an inter-

*We first heard this story from Robert Pike, Creative Training Techniques Int'l.

esting thing happened to most of the salespeople. By this point, they had heard nearly all the possible answers from prospective clients. They had become proficient at sizing up the personal and financial situation of the people they interviewed. Where it used to take 45 minutes or an hour to determine a customer's insurance needs, most could do it now in five or 10 minutes.

So, they stopped asking questions and listening. In fact, they moved into a "sales mode" very quickly and began doing more talking and less listening.

There was one problem: Prospective customers did not feel comfortable with this approach. A relationship did not have time to develop between the client and the salespersons, and neither gained value from the brief discussion. Sales invariably dropped off, while the salespeople wondered why their sales figures plummeted for no apparent reason. Then, they would get discouraged, making selling a more difficult task since they were focused on their fear of rejection or failure. Lowered sales impacted their self-confidence, and a downward performance spiral was in full gear.

What is the message? EQs build relationships among people. They are a gift to the person being asked them, just as the answers are a gift to the person asking them. When questions are no longer asked, for whatever reason, value is not derived and relationships do not develop to the same extent. EQs are as much or more for the responder as for the asker.

Typically in life, we enjoy the moments when we find clarity in our own explanations. These moments energize and empower us, because we see that we have the ability to find solutions on our own. Asking EQs gives leaders—in the above example, the salesperson is the leader—a method for generating such insights rather than waiting for those rare occasions when they occur spontaneously. Thus, EQs provide a tool for managing clarity and enhancing creativity as well as empowerment.

> *R*emember a time when you were explaining
> something to someone for the first time or
> even the tenth time. In either case, as you
> were explaining the concept got clearer for
> you than it ever had before. How did the new-
> found clarity make you feel?
>
> *H*ow was your energy affected?

Note: Often the process of probing for deeper under-standing and clarity requires more than one question. We will address this later in this chapter.

• EQs ARE YOU-ORIENTED.

EQs place the focus on the person answering. They ask: "What do *you* think we should do?" "What is *your* opinion?" "How do *you* feel about doing it this way?" "What was significant about that to *you*?"

No *wrong* answers exist for YOU-oriented questions, be-cause the answers are true for whoever is answering them. By the very nature of the question, the answers can only be correct. This factor removes the threat people may feel with other types of questions, particularly when there is no judgment about the responses. There is tremendous power in acceptance of people, and we send acceptance messages when we ask questions that cannot have wrong answers.

By asking YOU-oriented questions, we send a clear mes-sage about the importance of what each person thinks and feels. This builds cooperation, trust, and a climate that fos-ters deeply felt solutions.

• EQs GIVE THE ANSWERERS CREDIT FOR KNOWING THE ANSWERS, WHETHER THEY DO OR NOT.

In the typical business environment, many managers assume that people don't have the answers. Therefore, they cannot understand why questions should be asked at all. In such an environment, inquiries, at best, tend to be condescending and intimidating.

However, if we assume that people within the team really do have solutions and we ask to hear them, it is amazing how the creativity begins to flow. After working with hundreds of leaders throughout the country, the one statement we hear from our clients the most often—almost without exception—is: "I had no idea my people know as much as they do."

• EQs ARE OFTEN MULTILEVELED.

When asking EQs, we start with broad queries and move toward narrower ones. This additional probing steers people toward solutions. For example, we might start with this question:

> "What were you able to do today better than you have in the past?"

And then follow it with these:

> "What allowed you to do it better today?"

> "What did you learn about being able to do it better that you can apply to other areas of your work?"

Or, we can start narrow and move to wider applications, such as:

> "What are you doing personally that is working to produce better-quality widgets?"

"How could that approach be used in other areas
   of the company?"

Beginning inquiries should be easily answered and
should produce more general information. They should be
asked to empower a person rather than to force them into
answers that may result in their looking or feeling stupid
or inferior.

It is especially important to use a number of multileveled
questions to help people connect with the personal benefits
of their answers—the "what's-in-it-for-me" factor. A supervisor might ask a new employee, "What did you learn
today that pleased you most?" That's a good EQ, but when
multileveled questions are used, the answerer receives more
and more value. For instance:

"How does that fit in with what else you have
   learned here already?"

"In what way will that allow you to do even better
   tomorrow?"

"What are you most pleased about, personally, in
   learning that?"

"In what other aspects of your job could what you
   have learned be used?"

Caution: We need to be careful not to phrase multileveled
questions so they sound canned or appear to lead the answerer into a trap.

- **EQs SHOW PEOPLE THAT THEIR LEADER
  IS OPEN AND WILLING TO HEAR THEIR
  ANSWERS—WHATEVER THEY MAY BE.**

It is important for leaders to listen patiently to the answers to their EQs and to accept whatever they hear. This
is a test of a leader's openness and willingness to listen. In

initial stages of asking EQs, people may test us to see if we really want to hear whatever they have to say. Therefore, our reaction to every response is important. By demonstrating interest and openness, we begin building trust and developing more effective relationships.

To really mine the gold within an organization, leaders have to be open-minded. Be prepared to receive responses that are different than expected. Also, sometimes leaders are already clear and set on the solutions they think should be utilized—even before asking others for their solutions. If not cautious they may, therefore, negate the answers they get to their EQs. We can get stuck on our own pet remedies and not hear the solutions offered by, and asked for from the people who are closest to the problems we are seeking to solve. By being open-minded as we ask EQs, we might find that our people discover an even better solution than our own, or they might come up with the same idea. If they do, they will own it and make it work.

• EQs HELP LEADERS BECOME EFFECTIVE LISTENERS.

To paraphrase the timeless real estate principle, "location, location, and location," it is important to note that three of the most important factors in asking EQs are to "listen, listen, and listen." In the process of asking questions, we naturally tend to listen selectively while our minds race to the next question we want to ask. In doing so, we invariably miss something being said. We must learn to listen thoroughly until the response is absolutely complete before moving to the next question or level.

Many clients report that before gaining clarity on the value of EQs they did at least 80% of the talking and only 20% of the listening. Those who have learned the importance of asking EQs do 80% of the listening and only 20% of the talking with astounding results. This represents a shift toward Enlightened Leadership.

• EQs ARE FRAMED TO FIT THE SITUATION AND CLARIFY WHAT IS WANTED.

Framing, or setting up EQs appropriately, can be as important as the question itself. Framing helps set the tone or intention of the question. For example, "To gain a better understanding of how we stand on our project, let's first discuss the aspects of it with which we are most pleased." The basic question is, "With which aspects of the project are we most pleased?" The framing is the first part, "To gain a better understanding of how we stand with our project . . ." This sets the stage for the question itself. It helps people understand our motive and reduces their defensiveness.

Framing can also be useful when we are not clear about how to ask a question. For example, you may say, "I'm not sure how to ask this question, but . . ." and then ask the question the best way you know how. This is a way of defusing any issue that might arise from the way you ask a difficult question.

• EQs HELP LEADERS CONTINUALLY LOOK FOR WAYS TO EMPOWER THEIR PEOPLE AND TO MAKE THEM FEEL VALUED.

Leaders asking EQs must have as a guiding principle a question for themselves: "How can I help this individual gain more clarity or value in the process of answering the question?" "How can I balance the initial aspects of nurturing the people and creating the results?" We must remember that people have been asked questions in a negative mode most of their lives, so answering questions has probably not been very rewarding. Therefore, be patient as you change questions into an expression of trust, interest, openness, and solution-seeking.

TIMING IS EVERYTHING

As important as *what* we ask may be *when* we ask. For this reason, leaders also need to learn to be aware of the timing of their EQs. To make this point clear, let us look at an example.

We were going out to lunch with the executive vice president of a major health insurance provider in California. While we were waiting for the elevator, one of his top managers walked by. He asked how her team was doing that week. She replied that their productivity was up 20% again. He congratulated her as she walked off. Then he turned back to us and said that this was the third week in a row that her team had increased their productivity by about 20%.

We couldn't pass up the opportunity and asked him what would have been different if she had said that her productivity was down—even as little as 2%. His response was immediate: "I'd have called a meeting to find out why!"

Isn't that the way it usually is? Don't we call the meetings to find and fix the problems? Yet, the best time to call the meeting is while the team is on a roll. Instead of questions about what is wrong, imagine the power of asking questions like:

> "What are you doing that's allowed you to increase your productivity so much?"

> "What are you doing differently that is causing that to happen?"

> "What is working that we can apply to other areas of the organization?"

> "What are you most pleased with personally about what you have been able to accomplish?"

> "What could you do even more of to continue this trend?"

"What have you done to contribute to the team's success that most pleased you?"

"What could other members of the team do more of, better or differently to help you do an even better job?"

"What could I, as the team leader, do more of, better or differently that would help you do an even better job?"

The difference would be great between the way this team would feel returning to their jobs compared to the way they would feel leaving a typical "What's-the-problem?" meeting. And most of that difference could be summed up in one word—empowerment.

A STRUCTURE FOR EFFECTIVE QUESTIONS

In this chapter we merged the concept of questioning with focus to create EQs—"The Ultimate Empowerment Tool." When we express EQs in a generic form using the Framework for Continuous Renewal (or Continuous Improvement, etc.) as a guide, we generate a structured set of five questions that are often useful in accomplishing our objective of the moment.

We introduced the five-step Framework for Continuous Renewal in Chapter 6 as a particularly powerful focus tool. It is placed on the following page for review:

Framework for Continuous Renewal

1. Celebrate the small successes you are already achieving.

2. Research extensively what you are doing to generate these successes.

3. Continually reclarify (refocus on) in great detail the specific objectives.

4. Help all parties (customers, shareholders, the organization, team members, ourselves) understand the benefits of achieving the objectives.

5. Continually search for what you could do more of, better, or differently, to move closer to the objectives.

Below are the results of creating generic questions that follow the above framework:

Structured Effective Questions

1. What is already working?

2. What makes it work?

3. What is the objective?

4. What are the benefits of achieving this objective?

5. What can we do to move closer to our objective?

Notice how these questions align with the statement version of the Framework for Continuous Renewal. By putting the Framework in question format, we gain the additional advantages of asking instead of telling. This set of five EQs provides a basic structure from which to begin asking EQs in many different circumstances.

Like the Framework, questions 1 and 2 are empowering. They energize and open people up to their natural creativity. They encourage and nurture people.

Question 3 provides the opportunity to clarify (or reclarify) the specific, detailed objective(s). At this point, a gap is created between questions 1 and 2 together and question 3. It is this gap that we want to fill. When the gap is filled, the objective is met.

Question 4 helps us get in touch with the "why" of achieving the objective. This is the benefit—the "what's in it for me." At this point people buy in to achieving the objective.

Questions 1 through 4 prepare people psychologically and creatively to address what needs to be done to begin closing the gap. Question 5 generates the action plan that leads to a successfully accomplished objective.

Remember, the questions need to be framed and reworded based on the specific situation. This particular structure, this series of conceptual questions, can be utilized for many different purposes, including problem-solving, vision-building, professional selling, and project review. Chapter 11 discusses some real-world examples of using EQs.

THE MOST IMPORTANT ELEMENT

It is part of human nature to quest. Just as our mind is fueled by queries, every organization runs on questions. As leaders, we have the choice to settle for the questions naturally supplied by a somewhat negatively oriented culture or consciously replace them with questions that move our people effectively toward our objectives.

The examples we have collected through our work with clients provide overwhelming evidence of the power of asking EQs, yet EQs cannot be asked or taught merely as a "technique." Another aspect of the questioning process is just as important as the "technique" or wording or framing. This critical aspect of Effective Questions is the *intent* behind the question. No matter what words we use in a question, there are additional levels of communication that people pick up on. For instance, nonverbal information is communicated through our eyes, gestures, facial expressions, and tone. People will *sense* whether we are trying to support them in growing and being their best or trying to make them wrong about the situation.

> *Think back to a time when something was not going well in your organization and you were upset about it. Were you trying to support the team in being their best in the future, or were you really trying to find someone to blame for something that happened in the past?*
>
> *How do you think the team perceived your intention in that situation?*
>
> *How would their perception of your intention affect their ability to move forward in resolving the issues?*

Because the intention behind a question is so important, EQs provide an empowerment tool not only for those who are themselves already empowered. Indeed, it is not just the act of asking questions itself that empowers. The attitude of the person asking the question determines their effectiveness. The intention behind the question is critical, and a truly empowered leader will have a forward-seeking intention.

Remember, empowerment is a place to come *from*, an attitude or mindset, rather than something we *do*. We get

> *T*hink of the different intentions you could have when asking a question as innocent as, "What do you mean by that?"
>
> *W*hat intention would you tend to have when you are personally empowered at the moment of asking?
>
> *W*hat intention might you have when you are upset about something?
>
> *W*hat would be the effect of the question in the two scenarios?

a sense of someone's attitude in their communications. It's more than just the words they are using; it is a feeling, an essence. People *sense* where we are coming from. They *know* whether a communication is intended to "get" them or to help them. By being clear about your intent to bring value to an individual or team, you can use EQs to empower others while empowering yourself. As you make the gift of these valuable questions, you will be rewarded according to your intention.

Awareness provides the imperative element necessary for asking EQs. Awareness means knowledge, realization, consciousness, being informed. When asking a question, we must be conscious of, or sensitive to, whether our question brings value to the person being asked or whether it costs (hurts) them to answer.

Since intent is so important, we introduce EQs as a tool in our workshops only *after* the people have been through an empowerment process and a paradigm shift in awareness has taken place in the team. When people are empowered, they can be very effective with the questions they ask, and the words they use aren't as important. Their attitude says more than their words. The effectiveness of the questions depends upon the self-empowerment level of the person using them.

The *key* to renewal is the personal empowerment of the critical mass of people in an organization. Once leadership has become empowered, power can cascade rapidly down through an organization. EQs provide a tool for Enlightened Leaders to transfer this empowerment to their people.

USING EFFECTIVE QUESTIONS

Reactive Thinking 80%ers are naturally focused on *what's not working, what's wrong,* or *how they are going to be hurt.* This focus on the back side of the NeFER is ineffective in getting us to where we want to go. Yet, this way of seeing life is a fundamental state of mind of many people. To move them up significantly on the empowerment curve to Creative Thinking requires shifting this state.

EQs are the "how tos" we have been promising. As we begin utilizing EQs with an individual or team that is predominantly reactive, we interrupt their thinking patterns. In fact, at first this line of questioning might surprise them so much they don't even hear the question as it was asked. You might ask, "Pertaining to this particular project, what aspects of it are working best?" Don't be surprised if the answer starts out with, "The problem is . . ." If it does, just hear them out, acknowledge what was said, and re-ask the question—with sensitive reframing, of course.

In the empowerment process, what we are trying to do is support people in establishing new, effective thinking patterns to replace old, ineffective ones. The more we ask EQs, the more easily they can think in this new, forward-thinking direction. As it becomes easier for them, they begin to appreciate the different feeling of these questions and of their responses. They become aware of the value of this way of thinking and how much more pleasurable it is.

They notice they have more creativity, and they feel better about themselves and what they are doing. Their self-esteem is enhanced and attitudes are positively impacted.

At some point the pleasure of the new way of thinking is so strong they become clear internally (perhaps subconsciously) that they want more of whatever this is. When this feeling is internalized, they experience a paradigm shift in their way of thinking. Once this shift occurs, they will never go back permanently to their old way of thinking. Yes, they will slip occasionally, but the new awareness of the way it can be will help them keep coming back to this more joyful and effective paradigm.

Change-Friendly Highlights

1. Most organizations can make paradigm shifts literally overnight when leaders are able to tap into team members' deepest needs to feel empowered.

2. The shift begins when we recognize the need to dig below the surface, to touch the real issues, and to uncover the "What's-in-it-for-me?" channel, the one many people are tuned into.

3. The single-most valuable empowerment tool within any renewing organization is skillfully asked Effective Questions (EQs).

4. To succeed as leaders in empowering our team members, we need to become masters at asking EQs and effectively listening.

5. Structured Effective Questions are a five-step framework for focusing and aligning our people's energy toward achieving the organization's objectives. They balance the critical aspects of nurturing our people and creating results.

6. Just as important as the way Structured Effective Questions are framed, is the intent behind the questions. The leader must be empowered and clear that the intent of the questions is to support the person or team in finding their own solutions.

You cannot teach a man anything. You can only help him discover it within himself.

GALILEO GALILEI
Italian Astronomer and Physicist (1564–1642)

9

ALIGNMENT THROUGH SHARED PURPOSE AND VISION

Dreams, not desperation, move organizations to the highest levels of performance. Our dream ought to be institutions that work for, not against, our needs. This is the hope, the power, the dream, and the challenge in renewal.

ROBERT H. WATERMAN, JR.
Renewal Factor

WHAT ARE WE BUSY ABOUT?

When it comes to improving quality, customer service, productivity, sales, and all the other hard issues, we must recognize that people only apply themselves to the degree that they see the value of what they are doing. This sense of value grows out of their perception of the worthiness of their organization's purpose or mission and of how what they do contributes to that mission. To the extent they are clear about the importance of the team's mission and their role in it, their feelings of self-worth (self-image, self-esteem, etc.) are enhanced, and they put more discretionary energy into the job. If they are not clear about the importance of the mission or the significance of their role, their self-esteem is not served, and they will withold discretionary energy.

To illustrate this point, let's take a look at an East Coast company that won the bid for a relatively small project. Despite its small size, this venture was critically important to the firm's future; it would open doors and offer an opportunity for the company to become a pacesetter in a revolutionary new field. However, management experienced great difficulty getting people motivated to work on and complete this particular job. The company's employees were saying among themselves, "Why in the world did we take on this dingbat project? It doesn't make sense!" As a result, conflicts and subtle subversions were occurring on a daily basis. Productivity on the project was minimal, at best, and dissension was spreading into other areas.

During our initial team discussions, management began to realize that the team members did not fully understand and appreciate the reasons why the project was so vital. The team did not see its purpose or its worthiness and, therefore, had not bought in to the project. To generate discussion and greater understanding for both parties, management started asking the team members EQs. This opened the lines of communication, thus enabling the team members to grasp the project's significance. As they finally got a sense of the purpose and saw the project's long-term benefits both for the company and themselves, they willingly bought into the project and committed themselves to its successful completion.

Gaining people's alignment with a shared and worthy company mission represents one of the most critical aspects of a renewing, high-performance organization. The sharing of a mission or vision by all members of an organization directly supports the mindset shift to Creative Thinking and provides the forward focus of the powerful NeFER below. Alignment with a shared mission or purpose has a powerful effect on accessing and managing the tremendous energy and creativity already existing in our organizations.

Henry David Thoreau, the nineteenth-century naturalist and author wrote: "It's not enough to be busy; so are the ants. The question is: What are we busy about?" It is a fair question. We have discussed the factors involved in creating change-friendly and renewing organizations, but even if an organization is change-friendly and renewing, we must still decide in which direction to move—or, as Thoreau would say, "what" to be "busy about."

HIGH-PERFORMANCE CHARACTERISTICS

Renewing, high-performance organizations tend to have a number of common characteristics. One such characteristic consistently found to be critical in studies of high

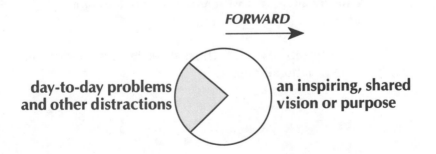

FORWARD

day-to-day problems and other distractions

an inspiring, shared vision or purpose

performance is a clear, empowering mission, purpose, or objective. Performance psychologist Charles Garfield says, "Peak performance begins with a commitment to a mission." He defines mission as "an image of a desired state of affairs that inspires action."

In their major study of high performance teams, entitled *Teamwork: What Must Go Right/What Can Go Wrong*, Drs. Carl E. Larson and Frank M. LaFasto found "consistently, and very emphatically . . . high performance teams have both a clear understanding of the goal to be achieved and a belief that the goal embodies a worthwhile or important result." They describe this characteristic as a "clear, elevating goal" and use goal, purpose, and mission somewhat interchangeably. Rather than getting tied down by terminology, for our purposes we will also use the terms interchangeably. The essential point is that we're referring to what we want to move toward and the reasons why.

Enlightened Leaders are clear about the importance of purpose, vision, and alignment to the renewing organization. They are clear about the criticality of having:

- **a deep, clearly understood sense of purpose or mission.**

- **a mission that incorporates a vision of what the organization stands for or strives to create what is inspiring and elevating to the team or organization members.**

- **a mission that is shared by the team members—causing alignment with and buy-in to a common objective.**

Let's look briefly at each of these three factors, beginning with the foundational one.

PURPOSE

Whether we are part of a Fortune 500 company, a professional baseball team, or an entrepreneurial venture, an internally bred purpose (the reason for which something exists or is done, or an intended result) clarifies direction and fuels the fire of achievement. Purpose gives us a reason to accomplish and a desire to do so.

Looking back at the "Framework for Continuous Renewal" and "Structured Effective Questions," Step 3 is the clarification of the objective. At the ultimate organizational level, our purpose or mission is that objective toward which we want to go. To the extent a mission is elevating or inspiring and shared by the individuals of the organization, it will create a gap that people are naturally encouraged to fill.

> *How would your team define its purpose?*
>
> *On a scale of 1 to 10, how clear and elevating is your team's purpose?*

VISION

Having an inspiring goal, mission, or objective as a point of focus keeps us on track. Often, however, organizational goals seem unexciting to our people. Thus, they wander off track, get distracted, or follow whatever may interest them at any given point.

Enlightened Leaders know how to get their people excited about their mission. By expanding the purpose into a vision, they effectively draw out the inspiring and energizing aspects of purpose so their people can become focused and excited about it.

Peter Block defines vision as: "Our deepest expression of what we want. It is the preferred future, a desirable state, an ideal state, an expression of optimism. It expresses the spiritual and idealistic side of our nature. It is a dream created in our waking hours of how we would like our lives to be." Thus, an organization's vision should embody the collective values and aspirations of its individuals. It should be a "mental image" held by the whole group and appealing to all its human aspects—physical senses, emotional needs, and spiritual quests. It is an expansion of the purpose or mission.

Vision inspires us to reach for possibilities and to make them realities. It brings out the best in ourselves and in our organizations. Vision helps men and women rise above their fears and preoccupations with what can go wrong and focus on what can go right.

In addition, a strong organizational vision encourages people to reach beyond their preconceived limitations and defensive barriers. When people's attention is drawn toward something bigger than themselves, like a clear and elevating goal, there is less energy and less desire available to focus on their perceived faults and limitations. They are pulled away from their personal, destructive worries and encouraged to contribute personally to a worthwhile cause—a focus that is empowering and renewing.

Remember those times when you were working toward something you really wanted. The people who told you the reasons you couldn't have it or do it became motivators rather than deterrents. Your determination was so strong that nothing could convince you that you could not attain your goal. You knew you could make your vision a reality, and this knowing allowed nothing to stand between it and you. In such a case, more than likely you achieved your goal.

Vision-building enables people to clarify what they really want and to get an image, a sense and a feeling of the way it could be. The gap that is created between *the way it is* and *the way it could be* naturally invites the creativity, energy, and commitment of people to bridge that gap.

When the organizational culture promotes a shared vision, then teamwork, effectiveness, and a renewal consciousness can flourish. People are eager to make that vision a reality.

ALIGNMENT

Alignment implies unified commitment. A team or organization is aligned when the members are individually and collectively committed to a common mission. Unified commitment is another consistent factor in high-performance teams and organizations. Indeed, we can't be aligned with the mission until we share it; alignment is a result of the *shared* part of the shared mission or shared vision. Unification assures that we are all pulling in the same direction.

People in aligned organizations are more lilkely to get along, no matter what pressures or challenges they face. Aligned team members generally keep their agreements with each other, because they possess commitment to an overriding purpose and vision. Aligned, renewing team members are also more capable of both constructively disagreeing about ideas and resolving these disagreements.

On August 2, 1985, in Broomfield, Colorado, two freight trains, both traveling 50 miles per hour, collided underneath a bridge of the Denver–Boulder turnpike in what became a national news story. There had been a switching mix-up, and both had somehow been diverted to the same track.

Five men were killed instantly. Wreckage was strewn everywhere. The fires were so hot that the steel girders of the turnpike bridge melted, collapsing the highway over the twisted mass of what had once been two trains.

That highway is a heavily traveled primary artery between Denver and Boulder. The Friday evening traffic became hopelessly snarled in both directions.

What happened in the next 48 hours proved to be nothing short of a gigantic, documented miracle. People in great numbers responded to the tragedy. Businesses, charitable organizations, construction firms, and governmental agencies became a united army.

Traffic was diverted and calls for help went out. High-intensity lights were in place within a short while, and emergency crews began working to pick through the wreckage. Construction work began within hours and continued around the clock.

A heavy-construction crew came from nearby Nebraska. Together unions and company management helped organize a virtual host of workers. Equipment was amassed from various Colorado suppliers. The Salvation Army and other organizations came on the scene with a mountain of food and a sea of coffee.

By Monday morning, a new highway was in place, down to freshly painted stripes. Even the railroad tracks had been replaced. By working cooperatively, this massive army of people overcame bureaucracy and barriers to accomplish in just 48 hours what would have normally taken four months! They did the impossible.

These people were fully operating out of a creative mindset—breaking out of boxes—moving past the "it's-not-my-job" syndrome and doing whatever was necessary to get the job done. The same thing can happen within any organization whose individuals are aligned toward a worthy mission. The synergy that accompanies alignment enables teams to do seemingly impossible things.

Developing alignment through purpose and vision is a primary renewing element, because it is a precondition for building organizational effectiveness. Once people are aligned, it is easier for them to reach agreements and to foster a working environment that helps everyone achieve their shared dreams.

THE POWER BEHIND VISION

Going through the process of defining a mission or vision encourages people to clarify both their organizational and individual values. The process has them clarify what is important to them and how what they want can be achieved through achieving the organization's vision. It allows them the opportunity to get in touch with "what's in it for me," as well as what's in it for the company, which brings an individual's purpose into alignment with the organization's mission.

Without a vision—an image of the way we want it to be—many of us tend to focus most of our attention on what's not working. By directing the energy toward correcting what is wrong with the present and focusing only on problems to be solved, we often lose sight of the ultimate objective in the process.

In contrast, having a vision inspires people to look at the possibilities of going beyond what is wrong and what, in the past, have been limitations. It pulls us to look at what *is working* and where we can go.

Consider the NeFER below.

Focusing on limitations bogs us down. A purpose or an expanded vision empowers us and pulls us toward the possibilities. When our focus is on *overcoming problems*, the purpose becomes to overcome the problem and more appropriate or already chosen objectives might be hidden from us.

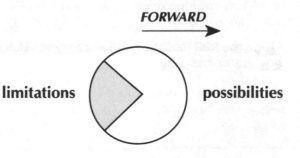

This was really brought to light when we were in Seattle the week before Christmas in 1990. Doug tells the story this way: "The weather was cold and the ground was icy and slippery. Ed and I walked out from a shopping mall one evening to get to our car, and I almost lost my footing on the first step I took outside.

"As we walked toward the car, I was being very careful not to fall. Suddenly, I heard Ed's voice calling from far behind me. Ed was standing next to the car. I had walked a whole parking aisle and a half past where the car was parked.

"Ed and I both left the store at the same time, with a clear objective—to get to the car. Ed managed to maintain that focus. Within that focus (on a primary objective) he also included a secondary objective of getting to the car safely. Without even being aware of it happening, I had become so focused on walking safely that I had lost touch with the primary objective and walked right past the car.

"While doing a very good job of what I *was* doing, it did not serve in accomplishing the primary objective. If Ed had not called out, I could have become so good at *walking safely* that I might still be walking."

Where might your team (or your organization) be falling into the trap of focusing so much attention on overcoming problems that they lose track of their primary objectives?

How clearly focused is your team on their primary objective?

What can you learn from this story that will help your team stay focused on their objective?

It seems obvious that people *should* be clear on what they are doing, just as it seemed obvious that Doug *should* have been going to his car when he left the shopping mall. Just because we are clear on an objective when we start out to accomplish it doesn't mean that level of clarity stays with us.

Often around our office one of us will be working on a project and get stuck. It still amazes us how quickly we can help each other get back on track with a simple question like, "What are you trying to accomplish with what you are doing?" or simply, "What is your objective?" These EQs quickly refocus our attention from wherever it is back to our objective.

> *What might be the value of occasionally asking your team questions like, "How does what you are doing fit into our objective? or "Describe what we are trying to accomplish."*
>
> *In what areas might your team be doing a good job of "walking safely," yet not getting any closer to its primary objective?*

By focusing on overcoming problems we tend to get mired in more and more problems. By continually refocusing on an elevating mission, however, we move toward our

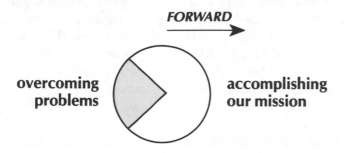

FORWARD

overcoming problems → accomplishing our mission

objective and simply handle problems as needed. Emphasizing the forward side of the NeFER, releases and focuses
the creativity, energy, and enthusiasm of our people.

Years ago we heard a story about three men laying brick
at a work site. All three had the same tools, mortar of iden-
tical consistency and materials that were alike. Yet, the men
somehow appeared different to an observer.

Curious, the observer asked the first worker, "What are
you doing?"

"Layin' brick," the laborer grumbled. "It's a paycheck
even if it is hard work."

"What are you doing?" the observer asked the next man.

"Well," the second worker replied, "I'm one of the construction people, and we are putting together the east wall
of a structure."

"What are you doing?" the observer queried the third
worker.

"I'm helping to build a cathedral," said the man. He
wiped his brow and spoke excitedly. "And someday right
where we are standing the spires will rise high above us,
and people will be meeting to worship and be educated."

The differences the observer noticed in the men were
variations in attitude. The first worker held a job. The second man had acquiesced to common goals. The third man
had bought in and become *aligned* with a powerful purpose
and vision.

By getting in touch with the personal value of an organization's vision, people see how their individual goals fit
into the organization's goals. Thus, the individual and organizational goals become aligned. In other words, both
individual and organization begin moving in the same direction toward a shared vision. People are empowered when
they are clear about how their personal goals are supported
by the organizational objectives, when they are in touch
with "what's in it for them" for doing what needs to be
done.

As leaders, we cannot assume people will automatically

see "what's in it for them." In *The Seven Habits of Highly Effective People*, Stephen Covey says, "You can buy a person's hand, but you can't buy his heart. His heart is where his enthusiasm, his loyalty is. You can buy his back, but you can't buy his brain. That's where his creativity is, his ingenuity, his resourcefulness."

If the first two bricklayers had been provided EQs, they might have discovered their own personal value in being part of the project and had a higher level of commitment to it. We cannot predict the personal benefit that individuals will perceive, and what the perceived benefit is, is not important. What is important is that they are in touch with it.

USING EQS TO DEVELOP PURPOSE AND VISION

EQs fit into the concepts of purpose, vision, and alignment perfectly. In fact, a structured sequence of EQs has proven to be useful in developing purpose and vision. When this approach is used with a team, natural alignment occurs because the purpose or vision is truly shared. The key is a multileveled approach to questions that gains individual participation, develops the mission, and gains buy-in from the team members.

Here is an example of who this process might proceed:

First Level:

"What are we doing that is already working well?"

"What are we best at?"

"What is our organization best known for?"

"What are our greatest strengths?"

"What is unique about us?"

Second Level:

"What is causing us to do well in each of these
areas?"

"What are our people doing best in each of these
areas?"

"What contributes most to our success?"

"What systems and processes particularly help?"

"What about these are particularly effective?"

The Level One and Level Two questions are focused on
what is already working. They put us in touch with the
positive aspects of our current situation and, therefore, are
highly energizing and empowering. They prepare us for
addressing the more creative and feeling aspects of our
ultimate vision by opening our minds and hearts.

Third Level:

"How would you describe the ultimate objective
for our organization?"

"If you overhear a conversation about our team
one year/two years/three years down the road,
what do you want people to be saying about
us?"

"What would it be like around here if you were
really excited about coming to work every
day?"

"If you could create the ultimate work environment, how would you describe it?"

"What would we be doing that would have you
excited about being part of it?"

The description of the mission or the expanded vision itself comes from the Level Three questions. These questions can be phrased many ways, and each configuration may help different members of the team gain greater clarity about what they want. Frame them in several different ways to pull out many perspectives.

The vision becomes shared through the participation process and through individual discovery of our own piece of the overall vision. In an advertising function, the Prudential Insurance Company has used this theme for years: "Own a piece of the rock." Belonging is important, but ownership of the overall vision is even more important to long-term success.

Fourth Level:

> "If we could achieve this objective—the vision of the way we want it to be—what would be the organizational benefits?"

> "If we could achieve this, what would it do for our team? For you personally?"

The purpose of Level Four questions is to gain buy-in. Buy-in is solidified as people get clear on the personal benefits of contributing to the cause. Once people understand how they will benefit from achieving their shared mission or vision, the available energy is enhanced enormously.

The traditional approach would have a manager say, "This is the new mission, and here is why we are going to move in this direction." At best this approach generates compliance or acquiescence, but the energy of compliance or acquiecsence does not come close to the energy and enthusiasm of ownership. At worst, telling people our vision generates defensiveness and resistance.

It is difficult to match the remarkable dynamics that occur when a critical mass of people in an organization become committed to and aligned with a *shared,* inspiring vision or mission. These dynamics include an exciting level of empowerment of the people, amazing availability of discretionary energy, extensive creativity, and a profound team synergy.

We can take the previous line of questioning one step further to include the following EQs.

Fifth Level:

"What do we need to do more of, better, or differently to achieve this objective?"

"What could I, as your leader, do more of, better, or differently to help you achieve this objective?"

"What two or three things can we count on you to do to support this vision?"

It is in this step that people take responsibility and ownership for what needs to be done—not because we told them what to do but because they have discovered it for themselves. This step develops the critical action plan. Without specific and appropriate action, the exercise is a lost cause.

Notice how these questions align with the Framework for Continuous Renewal (and Structured Effective Questions). An additional synergy is created when we use the empowering framework and pull the answers from the people through EQs.

Shared purpose and vision, and the resultant alignment, must come from the inner heart of an organization—its people. Through the use of EQs, the vision is discussed openly and is put into words, thus forcing internal accountability and commitment for later actions. Alignment through shared purpose or vision continually provides the forward side of the very powerful NeFER on page 183.

In the book *Leaders: The Strategies for Taking Charge,*

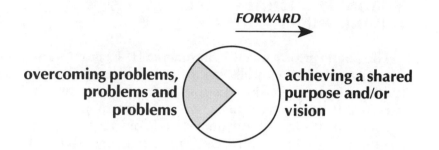

FORWARD

overcoming problems, problems and problems

achieving a shared purpose and/or vision

Warren Bennis and Bert Nanus write, "A vision cannot be established in an organization by edict, or by the exercise of power or coercion . . . In the end, the leader may be the one who articulates the vision and gives it legitimacy, who expresses the vision in captivating rhetoric that fires the imagination and emotions of followers, who—through the vision—empowers others to make decisions that get things done. But if the organization is to be successful, the image must grow out of the needs of the entire organization and must be 'claimed' or 'owned' by all the important actors."

Outstanding organizational performance and deep personal fulfillment work together and reinforce each other. These exciting results can only come through being clear on a purpose, sharing a vision and being in alignment. When in alignment, every system and technique becomes a vehicle for infusing the *spirit of renewal* into the organization rather than simply a mechanism that works only as long as leaders keep pushing or pulling them.

More than anything else, alignment through shared purpose and shared vision enables and empowers people and organizations to grow from the inside out. This kind of growth goes far beyond reducing resistance to change; it promotes renewal and builds a tenacious. vibrant spirit within individuals, teams, and organizations.

VISION OF A HIGH PERFORMANCE ENVIRONMENT

The High Performance Environment (HPE) is a working environment that naturally brings out the best in people. It does this by supporting the things that are important in our lives. If we, as individuals, are in an environment that supports the things that are important to us in most aspects of our lives—mental, physical, emotional, and spiritual, then that environment will bring out the best in us. We will be happy in that environment. We'll be energized in that environment. We will feel supported in that environment. Our needs, to a large degree, will be met in that environment; and we will put out a high degree of individual performance to support that environment. In general, such an environment will empower us to do and be our best.

In our workshops we also call this model or vision of the HPE the Desired Company/Organization/Team Environment. For example, if we were working with ABC Manufacturing Company, we would develop a vision of the Desired ABC Manufacturing Environment. When a team defines its Desired Environment, it develops a vision of the environment that would encourage it to be its very best, allow it to produce the most work, and support it in being the best it can be. By definition, it would be a mental image that appeals to its members' physical senses, their emotional desires and needs, and their spiritual quest. Thus, this vision would be quite empowering.

At a certain level, the vision of a High Performance/Desired Environment is predictable from organization to organization. No matter what team we work with, we can put its model of the Desired Environment side by side with another team's model and see that they are essentially the same. Over and over again, teams from varied backgrounds, diverse industries, different levels of education, and various levels of the corporate hierarchy—from the board of directors to the hourly factory workers—create a consistent vision of how they want their working environment to be. The words, some more sophisticated than others, may be different from team to team, but the essence is always the same.

In addition, in working with scores of teams we've found that every team already knows exactly what type of environment it needs to support high-performance work, to bring out the best in both the individuals and the team as a whole.

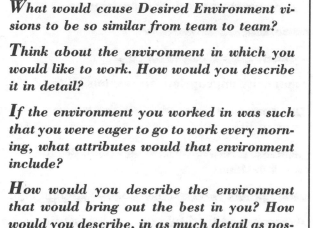

What would cause Desired Environment visions to be so similar from team to team?

Think about the environment in which you would like to work. How would you describe it in detail?

If the environment you worked in was such that you were eager to go to work every morning, what attributes would that environment include?

How would you describe the environment that would bring out the best in you? How would you describe, in as much detail as possible, what you would find in an environment that allowed you to be your very best?

If you asked your team members these questions, what do you think they would say?

List at least 10 aspects that would be important to you.

At a deep, fundamental level, we all want the same things. Some of the most consistent factors our clients tell us they want in their work environment, include:

- clear, common inspiring goals
- a high level of trust
- to be respected and appreciated
- a sense of team
- a comfortable, clean, orderly physical environment
- opportunity for input in decisions
- a solutions orientation
- people taking responsibility
- authority appropriate to responsibility
- a can-do, positive, winning attitude as a way of life
- encouragement to express creativity and try new ideas
- high priority on growing and developing people
- honesty and truthfulness as a way of life
- a place where management says what it means, means what it says, and does what it says it will do
- thorough communication based on integrity
- high quality in all aspects as a company standard
- freedom to do the job
- to be an example for other businesses of the way it can be

- adequate compensation and other rewards
- appreciation for the company and its people
- ability to set standards for the industry
- stimulating, challenging work
- freedom to "fail" or make mistakes
- responsive, caring leadership
- a supportive, warm, and friendly atmosphere
- people willing and eager to serve
- adequate resources
- a high level of professionalism
- empowered people open to change
- a fun, prosperous, growing workplace

Note: This list is so consistent that we have great confidence that your own team would create a similar list describing its Desired Environment. However, what's important is that the members develop their *own* shared vision of the way they want it to be. Showing them this list would not be effective! It would not be empowering for them, even though they would probably agree with the model.

Our intent in sharing this information is to raise awareness of the predictability of the model in order to support your confidence in asking your team to develop its own vision. When its members define their own Desired Environment, they will own it and will have much more interest in creating it. So, while we have discussed here the elements of the Desired Environment or HPE, it is important to pull out of your teams *their* vision in *their* words. And that vision should be the clear, general consensus of the team.

When they accomplish this, many of them will understand for the first time that all the team members really want the same things, which, in turn, will pull the people together into a stronger, more aligned team. Their Desired Environment becomes their "clear, elevating, shared goal."

> *W*hat would be the value of having your entire team clear about and sharing in the vision of the environment it wanted to create?
>
> *H*ow is the probability of being able to create that environment related to the degree to which your team participates in developing the model and is clear about what it would be like?
>
> *T*o what degree is its ownership of the environment dependent on its participation in creating the model itself?
>
> *O*nce they are clear about and in alignment with the shared model, how would this clarity and alignment enhance performance?
>
> *A*sk your team, "If we could create the environment here in which we'd most like to work, an environment that would have us excited about getting up and coming to work every single day, eager to be here, how would you describe it?" Have each person write down at least five factors before you begin to collect the ideas. Write them on a flip chart for all to see.

Just as we enjoy being around people with whom we feel good, we enjoy being in a work environment in which we feel good. Such an environment brings out the best in us because it supports who we are and our needs, desires, and values. It supports the things that are important to us.

Purpose or mission, vision, and alignment are soft, mind-set issues. Yet, when a team establishes the Desired Environment as its shared objective and common vision, a tremendous opportunity presents itself for gaining dramatic results in measurable, hard aspects of the business. These measurable results will occur as a fallout, as a result of moving closer and closer to such an inspiring, fulfilling vision.

Change-Friendly Highlights

1. Renewing, high-performance organizations and their leaders are discovering these critical factors:

   • There is a need for a deep, clearly understood sense of purpose or mission.

   • This mission must be inspiring, elevating to the members of the team or organization.

   • There must be alignment—team members have to buy in to that mission.

2. A shared purpose and vision and the resultant alignment must come from the inner heart of the organization. The key to unlocking that door is asking EQs and listening.

3. Outstanding organizational performance and deep personal fulfillment work together and reinforce each other.

4. A detailed description of the desired organizational environment, generated by the people, can provide a powerful shared vision to move toward in alignment.

Where there is no vision, the people perish.

Bible, King James Version
Proverbs 29:18

10

RENEWAL IN THE REAL WORLD

The best way to predict the future is to create it.

PETER DRUCKER

PRACTICALITIES

The concepts, disciplines, and tools explored in this book mean little unless they are put to use. To offer a better understanding of how to apply them, this chapter provides typical business scenarios. We have also suggested example NeFERs and EQs that may help clarify how these tools can be utilized effectively in the real world of business.

RENEWAL IN QUALITY

The quality challenge represents not a statistical issue but rather an attitudinal one. Unless people experience a shift in thinking about quality, the purported greatness of any new quality program has a limited chance for success.

Many quality problems grow out of a lack of commitment or an "I-don't-care" attitude. This mindset is fostered when people do not fully understand the organization's purpose and vision and how they fit into these pictures—or what they do understand does not inspire them. In addition, they may not see clearly what continually improving quality will do for them personally, so they do not even look for ways to do so. The bottom line to this issue is that our employees do not feel good about what they are doing, and they likely are stuck on the backward side of the NeFER below.

By not feeling that they are part of something important,

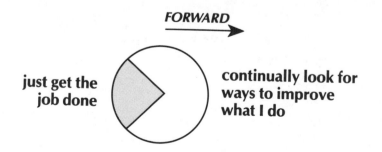

people are left in a disempowered state of mind. In this mindset, which probably is natural to more than 80% of them, their energy is limited, making little of it available to focus on making improvements. In this paradigm, it is more natural to fix blame than to seek solutions to quality problems, for this is a way to feel more powerful and protect themselves from being seen as the cause of the problem. When people don't feel good about their situation they may begin resenting it, which can lead to feelings of anger and hostility. When these emotions become strong enough, employees may even sabotage quality efforts.

Renewal in quality requires a shift in thinking to what we call Total Quality Consciousness, which is one step beyond Total Quality Control or Total Quality Management. When people come to work with a *consciousness*, or awareness, of the importance of quality and a desire to improve it in all aspects of their work, quality will improve.

This shift in thinking from "just getting the job done" to quality consciousness must occur to assure our ability to continuously improve products and services. For this to happen, the importance of quality must be a clear part of the organization's vision. Furthermore, it must be our people that declare its importance.

When vision is being discussed, questions need to be asked to generate discussion, such as, "How does the whole concept of quality fit into our vision?" "In what ways is quality important to us?" "How does quality affect our customers? Our company? Us as individuals?" Then, we must listen to all our people's different perspectives without judging them and let them come to their own conclusion about the importance of quality. No matter how long it takes, we must let them get clear about it for themselves before even considering what we could do to make quality better.

No amount or use of statistics will improve quality until a critical mass of our people experiences this paradigm shift in focus. However, Statistical Process Control is an important tool for validating the value of changes that affect quality. Once the attitudinal shift has occurred in people, they will be eager to use any and all tools to support their continued success. Without the shift, they are likely to resist the use of any tools. Enlightened Leaders know the key to quality is the mindset, or consciousness, of their people focused on continual quality improvement. The improved statistics are the result of that paradigm shift and the behavior that follows.

The several NeFERs that follow apply to quality environments and provide models for the choices we have about where we need to focus our attention and energy.

> *Does your organization typically deal with the symptoms (such as a bad product), or does it deal with the real issues (the process problems)?*
>
> *What message might people be receiving about the importance of quality when we continue to fix bad products instead of fixing the processes that made them bad?*

Not only is it important to deal with fixing the processes instead of the products, but while dealing with the process it is critical that people feel we are working on *process*

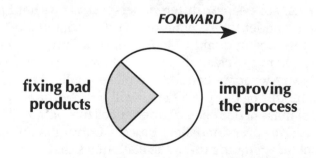

problems not on the *people*. The first NeFER below suggests the appropriate direction of our focus.

The second NeFER below shows a very critical choice we have discussed relating to defects vs. yields.

Does your organization focus on (eliminating) defects, or do you spend more energy on increasing the yield of good products?

Are your SPC charts graphing yields or defects?

How does this affect the focus of the people?

During the past five years, we have heard an increasing number of executives say, "The 'zero defects' program is a

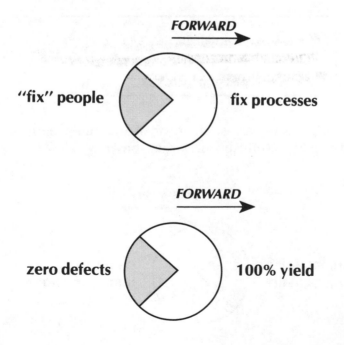

great idea, but it just hasn't worked for us." The reason it doesn't work relates to the focus issue. Focusing on zero defects spotlights defects in general. It is like the Karl Wallenda illustration—the tightrope walker died when he shifted his focus from "get to the other side" to "avoid falling." Focusing on avoiding falling is like focusing on eliminating defects. It puts all our energy squarely into defects, which is not what we want. We want better yield. Since we tend to get more of what we focus on, we need to focus on increasing yield. This is a subtle, but vitally important, shift.

The organizations we encounter that are increasing quality on a continuous basis are focused on *yield,* not defects. They know they will get more of what they focus on. If you question this concept, turn it around in your own organization and watch what happens, *with the proper intention*—no matter how well you think you are already doing!

Another NeFER for quality is shown below.

> **D**oes your organization seem to settle for maintenance or does it truly strive for greatness in the area of quality?

If your people are settling for maintaining the quality, productivity, or effectiveness that they have already, more

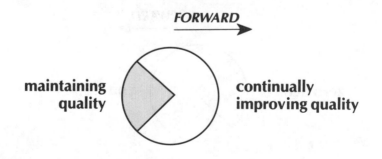

than likely they are not being pulled forward by a shared vision of how much better it could be. Work with your team to develop a vision of the way they want it to be. While doing so, have an interactive discussion about the importance of quality in that vision. Use questions like those found at the end of this section.

A quality NeFER:

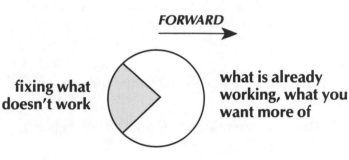

FORWARD

fixing what doesn't work

what is already working, what you want more of

> *Do your people focus more on what's wrong with the way it is or on what they want more of?*
>
> *Do you often see people mired in a problem, or do they quickly shift into a solutions orientation?*

Experiment with this NeFER. Surprise your team in your next meeting by focusing on what is working and what you could do more of. It might shock them at first, but watch the energy in the room. Start out the meeting with a simple "meeting opener" like, "Tell us something that has happened in your area of responsibility since our last meeting that you are particularly pleased about."

Here are some examples of quality-oriented EQs that may be useful in generating the focus that we desire:

"In what areas are we particularly pleased with our quality?"

"What are we doing in those areas to have the level of quality we do?"

"How would you describe the environment we will have when quality is where we want it?"

"What would it do for our customers if we could achieve those levels of quality? What would it do for our company? Our team? Each of us personally?"

"What can we do to make the process even better?"

"How could we utlitize this information better in other areas?"

"What could we do more of, better, or differently to get even closer to our quality objectives?"

These questions encourage thought, creativity, and participation in solutions. They tend to empower people toward Total Quality Consciousness. Notice how these questions align with the Structured Effective Questions in Chapter 8 and the Framework for "Continuous Quality Improvement" in Chapter 6. They start out with reframed versions of "What is already working?" and go through each of the five steps, ending with reframed versions of "What could we do to move closer to our objective?"

For a complimentary copy of "Enlightened Leadership: The Heart of Quality," call 1-800-798-9881.

RENEWAL IN CUSTOMER SERVICE

No matter how we ask the question "What is the real purpose of our business?" we invariably receive the answer "To serve the *customers*." Tom Peters says, "There are only two reasons for being in business; to serve the customer and to stay in business so we can serve the customer." This statement represents an intellectual paradigm held by much of the business world today. However, it is often only "intellectual" among the critical mass of an organization's people. Intellectual means they have heard expressed that it is important, but, since they haven't yet had a personal experience or feeling of it, they haven't yet bought in to the idea that it is *really* the purpose of the business.

> *On a scale of 1 to 10, 10 being the highest, what do you feel is the level of buy-in among your people in regard to customer service being the #1 priority?*
>
> *In what ways do you send subtle messages to your people concerning what you think about this issue?*

Let's look at it from a different perspective. Writes Paul Hawken in *Growing a Business*: "The customer comes first? Not really. The employee comes first. Employees' attitudes toward customers reflect their treatment by their employers. They cannot serve unless served. There's no way to instill a positive customer service ethic before you embody a positive employee ethic. Responsiveness in, responsiveness out."

The level of service an employee brings to a customer is a reflection of how well that employee feels "served," how well his or her needs are being met by the organization. To a large extent, the perception about this issue is determined by the relationship leadership has with the people in the organization.

So, which point of view is right? Are customers or employees more important? The answer to that is probably clear in each person's mind, but likely different from one person to another. Which is "right" is not nearly as important, however, as teams of people discussing the subject and reaching an agreement about their beliefs and how they want to handle this issue in the workplace. Whatever they reach agreement about is what they will commit to supporting.

We happen to think both points of view are right. Customers are most important. Yet who really are the customers? Who is the real customer for an individual team member or department? Are not their customers any person or department to whom they directly supply their product or service? For example, if I am a team member who receives an assembly and adds parts to it, the person who provides me with the assembly is my supplier and I am his or her customer. When I have added my value (the parts I install), I pass the assembly on to the next station. The person at the next station is my customer. The true customer for most employees of an organization is another employee.

In this scenario, the customer and the employee are the same. Furthermore, we can only serve the outside customer to the extent we serve each other. If I do not do a quality job in serving my internal customer, his or her job can be much more difficult and maybe even impossible to do in a quality manner. The better job I do in serving my customers, the easier it is for them to do their job, and so on down the line. Eventually, the *external* customer will be served according to how we have served each other internally.

To be able to serve our customers (internal or external) better, we must continually strive to understand their needs. In this ongoing process, EQs can serve us well. We should ask questions of our customers on a continuous basis like:

"What two or three things do you like best about our service (or products)?"

"If we were providing the ideal service, how would you describe it?"

"What could we do to take care of your needs even better?"

"In what ways would this improvement be most beneficial to you and your company?"

Two similar NeFERs that apply to customer service are shown below.

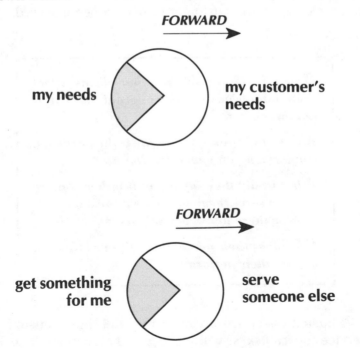

When we are stuck in a mindset of dealing with our own needs, little energy is available for satisfying the needs of either our external or internal customers. Thus, we must feel nurtured by others and okay with ourselves first, before we can shift our attention to serving others. The other side of the coin says that when we are focused on serving others because we *want to*—not out of feelings of sacrifice or obligation, our own needs will automatically be served.

Zig Ziglar, author and motivational speaker often called America's Salesman, says, "You can get anything in the world you want, if you just help enough people get what they want." Truly empowered people have come to realize that they are rewarded abundantly to the extent they serve others. There is a fine line, however, between a paradigm oriented to seving for the purpose of "gaining" and one oriented to serving for the sake of the pleasure gained in the process. The difference in intention between the two is felt clearly by the customer or person being served.

How would each of these paradigms affect the relationships of both internal and external customers?

What would your people say is the paradigm from which you generally operate?

What would they say about whether you are there to serve them and to help them do their jobs or there in a more self-serving mode?

How does their perception of your intention impact their performance?

A customer-service *program* may fail, but a customer-service *consciousness* will succeed and perpetuate. The difference is staggering and, as always, starts with the service provided by leadership.

> *What would it mean for customer service if the leaders in your organization could improve in their approach to serving their team members?*
>
> *How could the tools in this book be utilized to enhance this service to team members?*

To the extent our people feel supported, encouraged, nurtured—served—they will serve their internal/external customers.

RENEWAL IN CONTINUOUS IMPROVEMENT

Many leaders with whom we have worked experience frustration with all the excuses their people give for not achieving their goals. They didn't realize how natural it is for the majority of the people—the Reactive 80%ers—to focus in this defensive manner. Leaders play a critical role in refocusing their people in a more productive direction.

These NeFERs offer examples of the focus choices we might utilize to shift the ineffective, natural orientation of many of our people:

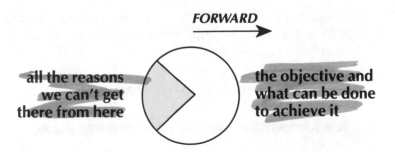

FORWARD

all the reasons we can't get there from here

the objective and what can be done to achieve it

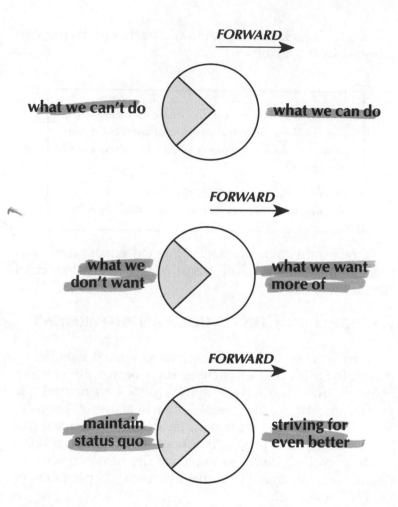

The Structured Effective Questions we have discussed previously work well for improving any focus situation. Slightly enhanced, they are:

Structured Effective Questions

"In this situation, what is already working? What else?"

> *What would be the benefits to your organization if the majority of its people were focused consistently on the forward side of these NeFERs?*
>
> *In what ways could you support your people in focusing forward on these NeFERs?*
>
> *What specific EQs might be useful for these NeFERs?*

"In those specific areas, what is causing it to work?"

"How would you describe in detail the way we want it to be? Or, what are our specific objectives? Specifically, what do we want to accomplish? What else?"

"What would be the benefits to the organization of achieving this objective? What would it do for our team? What else? For you personally?"

"What two or three things could we do now to begin moving toward this objective? What else?"

RENEWAL IN SALES

In the old paradigm, the sales motive was to address the customer's needs only enough to get the sale. In the new paradigm, developing a long-term relationship between company and customers is seen as a requirement for continuous renewal. The new sales paradigm aligns with the win-win philosophy, allowing or, perhaps, requiring both parties in the relationship to gain something.

According to Larry Wilson in *Changing the Game: The New Way to Sell*, a trend has appeared in buyers' needs. Our clients validate this trend, particularly in the capital-equipment arena. Customers want:

- An adequate solution—not necessarily all the "bells and whistles" but something that gets the job done.

- A trusted consultant with whom they can work and interact.

- Value-added quality—additional value for their money.

- A long-term relationship, rather than jumping from vendor to vendor.

Added together, the four parts of this trend suggest that people are not just looking for quality products or services but quality relationships as well. Three of the four elements are relationship oriented.

Once again, asking EQs in the sales arena is invaluable for developing relationships. Remember the story about the insurance company that noticed that the average sales-person's sales began dropping off after 18 months. You may recall that the decline occurred when the salespeople felt they had heard all the answers to their questions and, therefore, stopped asking their customers questions. When they weren't asking questions, the prospective customers were not receiving the personal value of the questions, and effective relationships were not developing. Customers could feel the difference and sales invariably dropped.

In today's and tomorrow's rapidly changing marketplace, relationships are more important than ever. Buyers are looking for long-term relationships, marriages rather than affairs.

Consider the sales NeFERs below.

People buy for their own reasons, not for ours; therefore, our sales success is related to discovering and keeping in touch with their reasons. Also, remember that their reasons may change. The reason they bought something yesterday may not be the same one that fuels their purchase today or tomorrow. Using EQs can help us uncover their true needs.

People buy benefits rather than services or products. They purchase what the service or product is going to *do* for them. Using EQs can tap into our customers' desired benefits and help them internalize the value of their decision.

If we were to ask,"Well, what's the problem with your current computer system?" the tendency might be for the buyer to get defensive and respond, "There's no real problem with what we have. We are just looking around." But if we asked Structured Effective Questions, we would likely

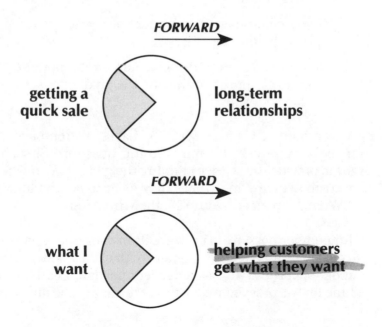

get very different results. They work extremely well for
encouraging people who may be somewhat reluctant to talk
about issues to reveal important information.

Appropriate EQs to use in such situations might be similar to these:

> "What do you like about your current system,
> product, or service?"

> "Regarding those specific areas that you like,
> which are most beneficial for you?" (Keep ask-
> ing "What else?" to get them to tell you every-
> thing they like about their current system,
> product, or service.)

> "What do you need from a product or service that
> you feel you aren't getting now? What would
> be even better for you?" (Use more "What
> else?" questions to develop the priority for
> critical issues.)

> "If you could have that product or service, what
> would be the benefits?

> "What two or three things could we do now to
> move closer to your having the product or ser-
> vice you want?"

When using EQs in a sales approach, it often becomes
unnecessary to ask the final closing question. Since we
want to provide the service of filling the gap between where
our customers are and where they want to be, the answer
to, "What do we need to do to get there from here?" becomes
obvious.

Remember not only to utilize EQs in your sales approach
but also to be an effective listener. With each answer comes
another opportunity to ask a deeper question. Leave plenty
of time for the prospective customer to answer the questions
fully.

A pitfall of the old-fashioned sales approach was the salesperson *telling* prospective purchasers *why* they should buy. As professional salespeople, we look for *client*-perceived gaps—not *seller*-perceived—between where they are now and where they want to be. We can do a great service by helping our customers get clear on their needs and desires. By getting customers to talk about what they like and want, we also help build strong relationships.

Plus, when we involve people in solutions, we tap into one of the greatest sales secrets of all time: People generally do not resist their own ideas; they buy into them. So, by using EQs, we can help them come up with their own ideas about what needs to be done, or what they need, making it unlikely that they will oppose those conclusions. However, if we come in as salespersons and try to tell them what they need, there usually will be natural resistance—the telling-versus-asking difference.

People buy where or from whom they feel understood. If they believe that we understand their needs, then they will be far more likely to buy from us. Asking EQs sends a clear message that "I care!" and want to understand.

What questions can you and your people ask to help your customers "want to buy" so that you won't have to sell them?*

**Note:* We have written an article about "Committee Selling," perhaps the most difficult kind of all, which describes the use of these concepts when seeking to gain agreement of a group. See last page of book for how to get a free copy.

RENEWAL IN PROBLEM-SOLVING

To summarize the use of the concepts and tools we have discussed to revitalize organizations and their people, let's look at the use of them in the area of problem-solving. This is perhaps the situation where the essence of all this material shows up.

You might be thinking, "I thought we weren't supposed to focus on problems!" Remember, this is absolutely not about ignoring problems but about dealing with them directly in ways that quickly lead us to solutions rather than getting us mired in the problem itself.

Structured Effective Questions are a powerful tool for dealing with issues in a way that brings out the best attitudes, energy, and creativity of people to resolve them. Let's review the generic questions:

Structured Effective Questions

1. What is already working?

2. What makes it work?

3. What is our objective?

4. What are the benefits of achieving this objective?

5. What can we do to move closer to the objective?

Notice that there is no mention of "problem" anywhere within these five steps. Yet, these five generic questions are a powerful way of quickly getting to solutions in a way that generates enthusiasm and commitment of the people to make it work. Let's look at a client story to show what we mean.

Quinton Instrument Company, a subsidiary of the American Home Products company located in Seattle, Washington, is a leading supplier of medical, fitness, and health equipment. A number of Quinton people from different departments met to deal with a major problem they were having with their "Specials" procedure—the process by which they respond to their customers' special (nonstandard) product requests. The "Specials" procedure was not working well and often resulted in late deliveries to customers. The topic had become a pet peeve of many people, and much frustration had built up around it. Conflicts about the procedure were reaching unhealthy proportions.

The issue previously had been discussed numerous times using old problem-solving approaches, which had always created defensiveness, low energy, and no solution. Ron Stickney, director of engineering, led the discussion differently this time by using Structured Effective Questions. As he began the process, some participants who had not yet been through our workshop questioned his approach.

"Why aren't we dealing with the problem?" they asked.

"Bear with me," Stickney requested, "as I approach the problem differently." When they agreed, he continued.

During the process, Stickney asked questions like:

"While we are having problems with our 'Specials' procedure, what are some of the procedure aspects that are effective?" "What else?"

"For that particular aspect, what specifically makes it effective?" "What is it that makes it work?" "What more specifically?"

"Just what are we trying to accomplish with our 'Specials' procedure?" "How would you precisely describe the procedure's objective?" "What else?"

"If we could achieve those objectives, what would

be the value to Quinton Instrument?" "What
else?" "To the team in this room?" "To each of
us?" (Going around the room one by one for
answers.)

"What could we do to come closer to achieving
these objectives?" "What else?"

The result of the Structured Effective Questions process
was a revelation! To the surprise of all, even though they
had been struggling with this problem for many months,
they discovered as a group that the most critical problems
were *not* the "Specials" procedure at all. The two biggest
problems were: (1) the existing procedure was sometimes
not being followed, and (2) the procedure was frequently
being used in ways it was not intended to be used.

With this discovery, the group quickly reached agreements that solved a major problem by dealing with the *real*
issues. As a bonus to the process, they even came up with
some good ideas for improving the "Specials" procedure
itself.

Stickney gives credit to the Structured Effective Questions approach for unlocking the creativity of the group.
"The approach moved us past all the frustration and conflict, shifted us to a positive attitude, and pulled us together
to work on the issue as a team with common goals," he
says. Using Structured Effective Questions, the frustration
vanished, the problem was solved and everyone walked out
of the meeting feeling good about what had happened there
and about being part of it. They were empowered by the
process.

In response to another's concern about the amount of
time required to utilize Structured Effective Questions, a
client said, "If you think Structured Effective Questions
require a large investment in time to solve problems, try
the costs of not getting the problems solved." Another client
suggested this might not be the most "efficient" approach,

but it might very well be the most "effective" approach to issue resolution, because the issue gets resolved the first time. The approach optimizes both the ability to get to the *real* problem and the ability to utilize the best creative talents of our people toward solving it.

Stephen Covey expresses it this way: "I have seen the consequences of attempting to shortcut (the) natural process of growth often in the business world, where executives attempt to 'buy' a new culture of improved productivity, quality, morale, and customer service with strong speeches, smile training, and external interventions. . . . But they ignore the low-trust climate produced by such manipulations. When these methods don't work, they look for other . . . techniques that will—all the time ignoring and violating the natural principles and processes on which a high-trust culture is based." Effective Questions greatly expedite the natural growth processes of the people in an organization.

The essence of all the concepts and tools in this book is the same: how to bring out the very best in people and move them toward what needs to be done to have the organization and each of them individually achieve dramatic success, happiness, and fulfillment. It is about creating an environment for unleashing and focusing the energy, creativity, and personal power of people for the common good of all. EQs are the tool which provide the balance between empowerment and focus necessary for developing that environment.

Change-Friendly Highlights

1. The tools explored in this book are like any other tools in that they are only effective if they are used.

2. The new paradigm helps us to be more effective in every area of a company, including performance, quality, cost containment, customer service, continuous improvement, and sales.

3. Enlightened Leaders know the key to quality is the collective attitude of their people.

4. People will serve their customers to the degree that they feel served by the organization and its leadership.

5. Asking Structured Effective Questions provides a profound way to help everyone get what they want.

During the last few years we have witnessed the beginning of the transformation of the U.S. corporation. The shift [is] from managers who traditionally were supposed to have all the answers and tell everyone what to do, to managers whose role it is to create a nourishing environment for personal growth. Increasingly we will think of managers as teachers, mentors, developers of human potential. The challenge will be to retrain managers, not workers, for the re-invented, information-age corporation.

JOHN NAISBITT
Megatrends

11

LEADERSHIP IN THE RENEWING ORGANIZATION

The bottom line is that leadership shows up in the inspired action of others. We traditionally have assessed leaders themselves. But maybe we should assess leadership by the degree to which people around leaders are inspired.

DR. JACK WEBER
Professor of Management
University of Virginia

RENEWAL AND LEADERSHIP

The critical responsibility of generating and perpetuating the mindset shift essential to creating continuously renewing, change-friendly organizations lies almost solely with those in leadership roles. The success of these men and women and their organizations depends upon their ability to empower their people and to have them take responsibility and ownership for the organization's objectives.

The kind of leadership needed today is very different from yesterday's hierarchical management models. It takes more that just good management for an organization to prosper in today's environment let alone tomorrow's world. It takes a special kind of leadership—Enlightened Leadership.

LEADERSHIP PAST

In yesterday's management model it seemed necessary to control virtually every aspect of the organizational environment from what was done to who did it to how it was done. The manager was supposed to be the one with all the answers and the one who, therefore, made the decisions. The manager was the one who held all of the power— at least the positional power.

This is understandable when we consider that most traditional management roles have military roots. The first time people were brought together to achieve an objective collectively was either for hunting or for war, and this trend continued into the Industrial Revolution. When the unskilled laborers first came into the factories, someone had to tell them what to do and how to do it. There was a need for "scientific management" to employ large numbers of people in productive work. The only model we had for managing large numbers of people was the command-and-control structure of the military. As a result, this became the model for managing any kind of organization. "The command model, with a very few at the top giving orders and a great many at the bottom obeying them, has remained the norm for nearly 100 years [starting in 1870]," writes Peter Drucker, management guru and author of *The New Realities*.

The phenomenal U.S. industrial growth after the Second World War confused the issue by seeming to validate the way we were doing things. It appeared that the way we were managing our companies was working well. However, it has become increasingly clear that the complacency of U.S. companies has had a great cost, and we are paying the price of settling for, and relying on, "the way we have always done it around here" with continued loss of market share in the new global marketplace.

Dr. Deming says, "In the decade after the [Second World] War, the rest of the world was devastated. North America was the only source of manufactured products the rest of the world needed. Almost any system of management will do well in a seller's market. Success in America was confused with ability to manage." This method of management was never effective. Its ineffectiveness just didn't show up on the bottom line during a seller's market.

In this old, limiting paradigm one of the ways success had been measured is by the accumulation of positional power. Working our way up the corporate ladder, our goal became to get more responsibility, more good ideas, more knowledge, and more people working for us than anyone else. The more we accumulated, the more many of us felt a sense— albeit, perhaps, false—of power and of control. It felt good. It seemed to support our self-esteem. We wanted more.

It is easy to see how this drive for power and control has created much of the business structure in place today. These power/control–based structures, however, actually create separation between organizational functions dependent upon each other. They create and perpetuate the barriers that limit the ability to work well together across departmental lines. Yet, it is the ability to work *together* that strengthens an organization's ability to survive in today's more challenging marketplace.

When playing the corporate game of seeing who acquires more power, who is most right, who has the best ideas, and who is going to look the best, we become reluctant to take the risk of having people do anything outside of our direct control. Therefore, we become hesitant to delegate responsibility, and stifle the creativity and effectiveness of our people. We also become less likely to take risks ourselves and tend to rely on the perceived safety of the "way we've always done it around here." We seek the comfort of the established methods, policies, and procedures. We lock ourselves in our own boxes.

REVISITING THE REALITY GAP

By functioning within these power-based organizational structures and boxing ourselves—and our employees—into old ways of operating, we lose touch with our people's desires, concerns, and needs. A study conducted by the U.S. Chamber of Commerce, presented in Chapter 7, showed that the top three items rated most important by employees were rated least important to employees from management's perspective. This clearly illustrates an enormous gap between what employees want and what management *thinks* they want.

In 1987, *INC. Magazine* commissioned an employee survey of the INC. 500, the fastest-growing small and mid-sized companies in America. They discovered that employees in these companies are not only more satisfied but more satisfied for interesting reasons. The study showed that, while their pay and benefit compensation is considerably less than that of employees in large corporations, "what they miss in hard currency is more than compensated for in the soft currencies of human-resources management."

To succeed in the '90s and beyond, leadership must be aware of the needs of their people. The more sensitive they are to these needs and the more they do to support fulfilling those needs, the more they will be rewarded through the empowered, focused efforts of the people toward the common good of all.

An example speaks to the importance of leaders being sensitive to the needs of their people and responding to those needs. Just about every basic management course will recommend that supervisors should acknowledge their people in front of their peers and give correction in private. Yet when Terry McElligot, maintenance supervisor at a plant in the Pacific Northwest, tried this approach of praising his people in meetings, he got a very negative response.

After meeting with them, he realized the issue had to do with low self-esteem. In fact, it was so low that when he acknowledged someone in a meeting, the person acknowledged was embarrassed to be singled out. That person's response was to feel worse about him- or herself. The rest of the team felt resentment for the person acknowledged, which resulted in further lowering the level of cooperation. There was no way the supervisor could win by applying what most people would agree is the proper "technique."

Following this realization, Terry began praising and acknowledging his people individually and in private. Imagine the impact of being called into your supervisor's office to be told what you were doing that he liked!

As Terry demonstrated, leaders must be aware of their impact on people and adjust their behaviors accordingly.

LEADERSHIP TODAY

According to some of the key names helping to shape the future of America, such as Peter Drucker, John Naisbitt, Tom Peters, Warren Bennis, Peter Block, and W. Edwards Deming, some unmistakable patterns are transforming our most basic assumptions about leadership. For example, currently leadership itself is one of the most challenged institutions in our society, whereas in the past leadership was highly touted. In recent Lou Harris polls, public opinion concerning leadership was reported to be at an appalling level. Of the adults questioned in one survey, 55% expressed feelings of alienation from those in leadership positions, and only 18% felt they could count on business brass, while just 14% said they still trusted labor union leaders.

Our educational systems constantly are challenged to deal with the issue of leadership. MBA programs are being asked to produce more pragmatic graduates who not only possess a knowledge of the world of business through numbers but who also understand what it means for a company to have a "social conscience" and a "team mentality" as well as know how to deal with "the people side" of leadership—phrases hardly ever spoken in the upper echelons of management before now.

Educating future organizational leaders in these subjects is imperative for businesses today. It is a totally new game compared to what it was even just a few years ago. The old rules and tools leaders used successfully in the past make sense only for a shrinking portion of the business community. A new set of leadership practices are needed that benefit from history but are not biased by the assumptions that shaped yesterday's management and leaders.

According to Naisbitt, author of *Megatrends 2000*, leadership during the coming years will move toward decentralization, and more decisions will be made at the lowest possible level. As a result, the classical management hierarchy will be turned upside down. And there will be no turning back to authoritarian systems.

"This effort at pushing responsibility downward is a direct assault on the bureaucratic methods and mindset that characterize life in most organizations," says Peter Block in *The Empowered Manager*. The bureaucratic approach is to hold on to the power. You cannot drive responsibility down without providing the power and authority—letting go of some of the control—at the same time.

In his article, "Lead Now or Forever Rest in Peace," David Altany reports, "rarely have even the most spectacular successes [in raising productivity efficiencies] tapped the full potential of companies . . . human resources." He goes on to say, "The determinant of success in the '90s will be how well companies motivate and *empower* the people they employ."

Yankelovich talks about the same thing when he says, "Our productivity as a nation . . . depends on how well we mobilize our discretionary effort."

This information is not new to most people in management roles. Indeed, the concepts themselves have grown threadbare from overuse. Yet, statistics seem to repeatedly point out that, while the concepts may be well grasped intellectually by managers, and many can even say the right words to their people, these men and women are not walking their talk. These leaders are saying one thing and doing another.

Although many organizations still are firmly married to the old way of doing things, new practices and concepts are emerging that are qualitatively and radically different from the old practices. Many of these are still in the conceptual stage; others, like the ones in this book, are beginning to pour into organizational life, often fueled by the entrepreneurial or intrapreneurial spirit.

Industrial bureaucracies are slowly being replaced in renewing organizations by flatter structures. These organizations have fewer levels of management and place greater responsibilities on the individual. Each person, as a result, has greater power to make decisions.

The growing number of "box-breaking" leaders, though currently few and far between, will be vital in an increasingly tumultuous marketplace. These change-friendly innovators will be most likely to find new solutions to today's challenges, which cannot be answered by yesterday's methods.

Organizations that delay their evolution from the traditional top-down style of management to a more empowering style are creating obstacles that keep them from effectively managing change. In fact, the traditional management approach itself actually creates resistance to change among employees.

EXTREME LEADERSHIP STYLES

Traditional managers tend to focus more on hard issues than they do on soft issues. These managers deal with symptoms instead of uncovering the real cause of problems. They tend to have a compelling desire to find and fix what is wrong—the problem orientation that distracts from accomplishing the objectives. The more problems they fix, the more they will find. They may even create some while solving others. We call these traditional managers Reactive Leaders.

Creative Leaders, on the other hand, tend to balance their focus on the soft and hard issues, knowing the actual cause of problems is often a soft issue. They very quickly move from a problem orientation to a solutions orientation. They know the importance of the team's mindset, and they understand the impact of their own actions and behaviors on this mindset and deal with it accordingly. Creative Leaders support alignment with a shared purpose or vision that nurtures ownership by team members.

The leadership model on page 223 shows other factors delineating traditional hierarchical management, Reactive Leadership, from that leadership required to assure continuous renewal, Creative Leadership.

As with many models, this one represents extremes. As the 0–10 scale at the bottom suggests, this is a continuum. Everyone in a management role is somewhere on the continuum. Let us hasten to add that we have seen few, if any, zeros or tens.

ENLIGHTENED LEADERSHIP

The ultimate leader is certainly not the Reactive Leader, but neither is it necessarily the Creative Leader. The Creative Leadership style is not always the best approach for a given circumstance. For example, when a fire alarm goes

Extreme Leadership Styles

Reactive Leader

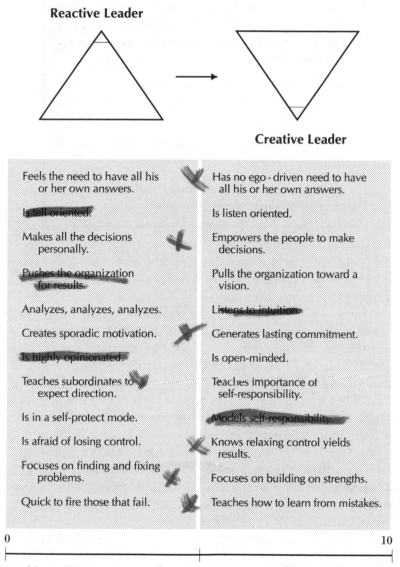

Creative Leader

Feels the need to have all his or her own answers.	Has no ego-driven need to have all his or her own answers.
Is tell oriented.	Is listen oriented.
Makes all the decisions personally.	Empowers the people to make decisions.
Pushes the organization for results.	Pulls the organization toward a vision.
Analyzes, analyzes, analyzes.	Listens to intuition.
Creates sporadic motivation.	Generates lasting commitment.
Is highly opinionated.	Is open-minded.
Teaches subordinates to expect direction.	Teaches importance of self-responsibility.
Is in a self-protect mode.	Models self-responsibility.
Is afraid of losing control.	Knows relaxing control yields results.
Focuses on finding and fixing problems.	Focuses on building on strengths.
Quick to fire those that fail.	Teaches how to learn from mistakes.

0   10

Note: Discovering where one is personally on this model should not be an attempt to judge one's self but rather to determine the direction needed for self-development.

> *Look at each of the Reactive-Creative Leader attribute pairs. Where do you think your people would place you on a 0—10 scale for each of these attribute pairs?*
>
> *In which areas could you improve to have the most immediate impact on your team achieving their objectives?*
>
> *In what ways could you make improvements in these areas?*
>
> *What specific action could you take today that would make a difference?*

off, it is appropriate to react quickly and decisively—the normal style of the Reactive Leader. Which style is most appropriate is situational.

There is a potential trap here, though. Many managers see so much urgency in *everything* that they are constantly fighting fires, thus justifying being a Reactive Leader. The 80/20 Rule of Thumb applies here also, so 80% or more of the managers in your organization may be more Reactive than Creative. Since this is the only mode many of them know, they might be perpetuating the fire fighting, because it feels more comfortable.

We feel "Enlightened Leader" is appropriate terminology for the ultimate leader. Such leaders know the true power of an organization lies within its people, and they continually quest for better understanding about what it takes to bring out the best in these people.

Enlightened Leaders are sensitive to the needs of people around them, and their responses vary according to the situation at hand. They have high versatility and move up and down the 0–10 continuum of our leadership model as appropriate to the situation. Enlightened Leaders realize that effective leadership is not about doing it one way or

another, or even being one way or another, but about being
aware of what is going on around them and making conscious choices about how to respond. They consciously *respond* rather than *react*. They are response-*able*. They
probably spend much more than 80% of their energy in a
Creative Leader mode and much less than 20% of their
energy in a Reactive Leader mode.

Joe Hood is plant manager of a high-tech fasteners manufacturing operation in Tucson. He is one of the more Enlightened Leaders with whom we have worked. While on
tour of his newly constructed plant, he was approached by
one of his maintenance people. Let's call him Bob. Bob
informed Joe that the Freon salesman was there to get their
start-up order. (Freon is part of their manufacturing process.) Bob said they needed to decide if they wanted to
order the Freon in 50-gallon drums and reorder frequently
or have a 2,000-gallon holding tank installed and use a
portable cart to move smaller amounts around the plant.

It would have been easy for a more traditional manager to
have immediately told Bob what to do. Instead Joe began asking Bob [Effective Questions] about the options and the benefits and the drawbacks of each choice. Even though there
were many disadvantages to the 50-gallon drums, Bob's responses kept coming back to them. Yet, it was clear that using
the 50-gallon drums wasn't the option he wanted to choose.

Again, a less empowering manager might have jumped
in with the solution. Not Joe. He kept asking questions until
Bob got down to what was keeping him from making the
decision he felt was best. Bob had heard that the budget
was a bit tight, and he knew that putting in the 2,000-
gallon holding tank was a major financial investment—but,
in his mind, this was the best choice. On the other hand,
they could buy the 50-gallon drums a few at a time as they
needed them and reduce their initial expenditure on Freon.

"If the holding tank is truly the best decision, how might
we work out the finances more favorably?" Joe asked him.

Bob thought for a moment, and then replied, "When I
bought my car I was able to make payments."

"Do you think that might be possible with the 2,000-gallon tank?" Joe asked.

"I'll find out," said Bob and quickly left.

When Bob caught up with us later, he said that the company could indeed buy the larger tank with installment payments, and he had worked out the arrangements with the salesman. The look of pride, accomplishment, and satisfaction on Bob's face was priceless.

Of course, results are what really count. After the plant was open only three months it was already weeks ahead of the projected production schedule. Furthermore, they did it in only 50% of the planned space allocation for this function. This is but one example of an Enlightened Leader who clearly knows how to empower his people.

In what ways have you been frustrated in the past by people coming to you for even simple decisions?

Considering the interchange between Joe and Bob, what might you do differently next time to better wean your people from running to you for every decision?

What would be the benefits for the organization? For your people? For you?

LEADERSHIP AND POWER

An inherent part of a renewing organization is that leaders work with the people around them and help them put into words their own vision of greatness for the future. Block wrote: "Our goal is not simply to have others embody our vision but to support others in embodying their vision. It is an expression of our belief that there is more than one answer. Often when we ask people what their vision is, they say that they don't have a vision. Don't you believe it. Each of us has hopes for a preferred future; it is just that we get so used to responding to others' expectations of us that our own vision remains at an unconscious level." Drawing out this vision and empowering people to move in the direction of that ideal requires inspiration; it requires leadership, not management.

To achieve continuous renewal, we must practice Enlightened Leadership instead of traditional management. What people really want and need is not likely to be provided adequately by someone in a management role operating from the classical top-down, tell-oriented hierarchy. It can be provided, however, by managers and leaders who do away with this top-down hierarchy and empower their employees.

Much of the core difference between the two approaches revolves around the use of power. Empowerment is giving away power and control while management is holding on to power and control. People who empower others have reached a stage in self-development where they no longer feel threatened by someone else having power. They are comfortable enough with themselves that they no longer need to hold on to the external reins of power in order to feel secure in themselves and in their positions. They come from a place of true personal power, which means having a high level of self-confidence and self-esteem, not just from a place of positional power.

Block says, "In order to create an entrepreneurial culture . . . we must give up some of our control. We can take comfort in the fact that we are only giving away something we never really had in the first place." Empowered leaders also know that giving away power, like lighting many candles from a single one, does not *subtract* from their power, but *adds* to it.

Today's organizations can no longer afford merely to be managed; they must be led, and people must be inspired to new levels of innovation, creativity, and achievement. It is somewhat ironic that while the burden for achieving this turnaround lies on the shoulders of our business leaders, the key to accomplishing the necessary breakthroughs is the sharing of that burden with their people. For many leaders in the old mold, making that change for themselves may be their greatest personal challenge in the '90s. Until they do make the shift in their own mindset, it is doubtful there will be much of a change in their people.

Unlike yesterday's cookie-cutter hierarchy, each organization must create its own model of what it will take to assure a prosperous future, and it will take real experts to develop that model for each organization. The good news is that each organization already has the experts—their own people. All we have to do is access the wealth of knowledge, creativity, and energy we already have within our people, and that is accomplished through Enlightened Leadership.

In 1985 a manufacturing company in Ohio was faced with a crisis. Fifty percent of their market had been seized by foreign suppliers. Not only were they being underpriced, but what took them months to deliver was sometimes available from offshore suppliers the next day. To be competitive they would have to reduce costs by 40%, increase functionality 40%, and develop the product in one year instead of the usual two. They finished in nine months, achieving all of their objectives. The next year they sold 2.5 times as much product as they had with their older model.

These breakthrough results where achieved by the people already working there. They were achieved by creating a team structure outside of the norm of that organization and by empowering people to reach beyond their own perception of limits. It took box-breaking, Enlightened Leadership to pull it off—leadership who knew the solutions were available through the people, leadership who knew that the key to outstanding performance was empowerment of the people.

This story can be re-created for any organization where leadership is willing to make the shift from the traditional top-down model of management to Enlightened Leadership—leadership that inspires people to amazing increases in effectiveness. People want to make a difference by contributing to solutions. They want to be valued for their work and feel important. People want to be part of a winning team. Enlightened Leaders are eager to create an environment in which their people can get what they want while creating extraordinary results for themselves and for the organization.

In his article, Altany says, "The leader's ability to enroll others is the key to achieving breakthroughs in a company. When a leader can inspire people as well as show them how they can contribute to his or her vision, people begin to expand beyond their previous limits. The bottom line is that leadership shows up in the action of others. We traditionally have assessed leadership by looking at the leaders themselves. But maybe we should assess leadership by the degree to which people around leaders are inspired. [True] leaders can make unreasonable requests of people, and have them fulfilled, because people are inspired."

AWARENESS—THE CRITICAL FACTOR

Awareness is the major differentiator between Enlightened Leaders and others. We grew up in the times of the "haves" and the "have-nots." Today, we are in the times of the "awares" and the "aware-nots." Some of the key awarenesses from which Enlightened Leaders operate include an understanding of the following factors about organizations, people, and leadership:

- **The most important factor in an organization's success is its people.** All the answers or solutions an organization needs are already available in its people. The answers are available conceptually through their knowledge and creativity, and they are available in actuality through their energy and commitment to having their own solutions work.

Enlightened Leaders create an environment or culture that unlocks the creativity and energy of the people, an environment that supports their natural desire to make a contribution and that has them *want* to make a contribution.

- **The behavior of leadership has a major impact on the people.** The Emerson saying, "What you are speaks so loudly that I cannot hear what you say," applies here. Talking doesn't count. What leadership "does" is what is "heard"—it is the "walk" more than the "talk." The only thing that really counts is the perception by the people of what kind of person the leader really is. You can talk about honesty all day long, but if your behavior is not congruent with the talk, people will not trust you. People are not likely to be any more self-responsible than they perceive the leader is.

- **People resist being told what to do, and they readily commit to making their own ideas work.** A primary problem with tell-oriented, Reactive Leadership is that people will naturally be resistant to the ideas of others. Even if the idea is a good one, it is often doomed to failure from the lack of commitment of the people who have to make it work. Enlightened Leaders know that people will wholeheartedly commit to having their own ideas work. These true leaders will go out of their way to have their people discover their own answers even if the leaders already have some good ideas of their own. They have developed enough personal self-confidence that they can let go of their ego-driven need to have all the answers and get credit for them.

- **To the extent people feel cared about and supported, they will go to extremes to help those who help them.** Enlightened Leaders operate with the knowledge that to the extent their people's needs and desires are fulfilled, they will go to extremes to serve the organization that supports them. Help people get what they want, and they will jump through hoops for you. Enlightened Leaders genuinely care about their people and want to help them grow and succeed as individuals. They know the truth behind a statement we have heard for years, "Your people don't care how much you know until they know how much you care."

- There is tremendous power in numbers. When a group of people is in an empowered state— energized, open, creative—and the group shares ownership of a common, elevating mission, the synergy that develops allows them to accomplish almost anything they really want to do. If that same energy is focused on a self-destructive path, the natural law works the same way.

Since awareness is the critical differentiating quality of Enlightened Leaders, what they *do*, the actions they take, are naturally influenced by questions they ask themselves about each of these factors. For example, Enlightened Leaders ask themselves (sometimes unconsciously) certain kinds of questions, which you might ask yourself.

The answers each individual leader has for these questions are the ones that will work! The following general actions, however, consistently surface in our workshop environments:

Consistent Enlightened Leadership Actions

- **Support people getting clear on an inspiring, compelling vision.**

- **Provide the positive disciplines necessary for bringing out the best in people and achieving the vision.**

- Put the people first.
- Model self-responsibility.
- Have high expectations for results.

> *How can I best create and support an environment that brings out the best from my most important resource and asset—my people? What else can I do?*
>
> *In order for me to send out the most effective messages to my people, what behaviors do I need to model? Which of these am I already doing well? Which do I need to work on? How can I determine what messages are being received? What else?*
>
> *In this (any specific) situation, how can I best help my people discover their own solutions as a team? What else?*
>
> *What kinds of things can I do to clearly show that I care for my people and am deeply interested in their success? What else?*
>
> *What things can I do to best empower my people? What EQs could I ask (in any specific situation) that would support this empowerment and focus? How can I continually encourage the most effective focus? What else?*

Let's review these factors in some more detail. Enlightened Leaders:

Support people getting clear on an inspiring, compelling vision. This is a vision of the way *they* want the environment to be, what *they* want to create. This should include a shared, elevating mission or goal.

Provide the positive disciplines necessary for bringing out the best in people and achieving the vision. The fundamental positive disciplines for continuous renewal are: (1) focusing forward on the NeFER and (2) utilizing EQs that both focus and "ask" at the same time. Enlightened Leaders see Structured EQs as a constant guideline in the process of mastering the art of asking EQs and listening. Enlightened Leaders run on forward-focused questions like:

"What are we doing that is working especially well?"

"What, specifically, are we doing to cause these successes?"

"How will this decision or action support our vision?"

"How could this be done in a way that would best support our people?"

"How would I respond to this situation in a way that best supports us moving forward?"

"What else could we do to move even closer to our vision?"

"In what ways could I better serve our team?"

Put the people first. Through caring about the welfare of the people and knowing their combined knowledge, creativity, and focused energy are what make an organization successful, Enlightened Leaders are sensitive to the needs and desires of their people. They interact with their people openly and honestly. They involve them in decisions that affect them.

Model self-responsibility. Enlightened Leaders take responsibility for failures and share credit for successes. They are quick to admit mistakes and readily say, "I don't know." They demonstrate the behaviors they would like to see from others such as trust, appreciation, caring, and concern.

Have high expectations for results. Enlightened Leaders are both people-oriented and results-oriented. They understand the criticality of balancing the energy put into taking care of the people and creating the results through those people. They readily accept *who* people are, but do not accept poor *behavior*, since poor behavior does not lead to effective results.

The responsibility for creating the environment that supports continuous renewal lies with leadership. Leaders must provide the positive disciplines that make it easy and natural to access solutions from their people. By modeling this forward-focused discipline consistently, the culture or environment begins to change. As more and more of the people begin following the lead and applying the same disciplines, a noticeable shift takes place. That shift in the environment, energy, attitudes, and performance can be felt. At the point that a critical mass of the people make the shift, the organization experiences a dramatic paradigm shift as well. Suddenly, the environment feels different, totally new. The difference shows up dramatically in the hard issues of performance—quality, profit, productivity, etc. This is true renewal.

LEADERSHIP IN ACTION

Alan Blackwood, a Hewlett-Packard executive, tells this story. "Tom manages a group of people in a centralized location who focus very intently on performing computer tasks both efficiently and effectively. They are process-oriented. Tom is intellectually brilliant and very analytical. By every statistical measure, the efficiency and effective-ness of that organization was extremely good and improv-ing. Tom was so intent on doing well at what he understood his job to be, that he drove his people mercilessly. His people were ready to revolt. More importantly, the internal cus-tomers he served, managers who needed the information that flowed from his group, felt like they were not well served. Tom was in danger of losing the support of his team and, perhaps, his job.

"When I [Alan] confronted Tom with the fact that many of his customers said that he did not understand their busi-ness, their needs, and did not feel they were getting any value added from him or his team, it blew him away. He was very sensitive to the need for 'data' but insensitive to the need for 'information' and interaction with his cus-tomers. He was doing a great job of giving them numbers, reports, graphs, etc., but not the analysis of that data—to turn it into information—that met their needs. He also didn't understand the impact of relationships with those customers and how that affected their perception of service.

"For example, a manager went to Tom and said that he had a problem, because he wasn't getting the type of in-formation he needed. The response was, 'That's not a prob-lem; here's the data.' That manager came back to me and said, 'Tom doesn't understand my business. He doesn't un-derstand what I'm trying to accomplish. He doesn't rec-ognize my needs. He just gives me more numbers to work with. He's not part of my team.'

"Because he had tremendous skills to offer, I decided to work with Tom. We began by using NeFERs and Effective Questions. Beginning with the use of the top levels of Struc-tured EQ [What's working? and What makes it work?], we worked together over a full day and a half. It was painful for both of us. For me because I could see his unrealized capacity to be part of the team and provide information. For him, because of the fear that he might give bad advice and be blamed. On the morning of the second day, he made the shift. What he suddenly realized and said was, 'I can do that!' I don't think he believed that before. When he reached that point of recognition and empowerment, then *he* started asking the questions. It was a paradigm shift.

"Tom immediately began to go to his customers, listen to their needs, and offer advice. Of course, that made them very wary. At first, every time that happened, customers would back away from him, which caused him to regress. But it was a real growing process for him. After some additional coaching, he experimented with how to interact with people in ways that built trust and respect. He soon began to have breakthroughs in key relationships with other managers, and, additionally, his own team members.

"His effectiveness is unbelievable today compared to where it was. On a scale of 1–10, he probably was a two based on his customer-service issues. Today he probably is a five or six and continually moving up. His customers are now going to him and asking his advice and asking him to be part of their planning processes. The mindset shift, the paradigm shift, that Tom went through was the result of three factors:

1. The fact that Tom discovered his own answers to the issues.

2. The recognition on Tom's part that he could and would be accepted as a trusted counselor.

3. His recognizing that he could ask EQs and discover what people's real needs were and what they expected from him.

"Tom's impervious, superman uniform has come off and he is growing. He has dealt with the feelings of fear that he had initially about the possibility of rejection, and he's discovered the personal satisfaction of being accepted. He was in danger a year and a half ago of losing his job. Today he's in danger of a promotion."

What was the cost to the organization of the time that Alan spent working with Tom?

What would have been the cost if he had not committed the time and Tom had been lost to the organization?

What situation do you have in your own organization that this story reminds you of?

What could you do to support turning the situation around?

What would a successful turnaround be worth to your organization?

Notice how Alan supported Tom in getting a clear, inspiring vision of what his job could be. The entire session with Tom was a process in which Alan provided the positive disciplines that brought out the best in Tom. With a major commitment of his own time, Alan clearly "put the people first." By demonstrating trust, appreciation, caring, and concern for Tom, Alan provided quite a model of self-responsibility. What an example of Enlightened Leadership!

Enlightened Leadership means balancing the need to take care of our people—our most important asset—and the need to create results through the effective leadership of those people. The critical balance is found between supporting the growth and development of our people through a nurturing, encouraging, supportive environment and creating solid, high-level results. It means meeting the social and environmental responsibilities within and beyond the organization. It means balancing the demands of today and the demands of tomorrow.

Change-Friendly Highlights

1. Only by sharing responsibility and authority with our people can we hope to have them take ownership for assuring a prosperous future for our organizations.

2. The transition from classical management to inspired leadership is the key to creating renewing organizations where people take ownership.

3. This will only occur when we extend power to others, when we begin to empower our people. This empowerment is the essence of true leadership.

4. The shift in attitude to an empowered mindset must start at the top in an organization for renewal efforts to be effective and successful long term.

5. If we are to succeed as leaders in empowering our team members, we need to become masters at asking EQs and listening.

Effective leaders give team members the self-confidence to act, to take charge of their responsibilities, and make changes occur rather than merely perform assigned tasks. In short, leaders create leaders!

CARL E. LARSON AND FRANK M. LAFASTO
Teamwork: What Must Go Right/What Can Go Wrong

12

THE BOTTOM LINE

Change—real change—comes from the inside out. It doesn't come from hacking at the leaves of attitude and behavior with quick fix personality ethic techniques. It comes from striking at the root—the fabric of our thought, the fundamental, essential paradigms, which give definition to our character and create the lens through which we see the world.

STEPHEN COVEY
The Seven Habits of Highly Effective People

INTENTION—THE CRITICAL INGREDIENT

This entire book, as well as our organization, is dedicated to developing the framework, disciplines, and tools for creating continuous renewal in people and organizations. When applied consistently and effectively, these tools work extremely well to create the paradigm shift in thinking required for renewal. What is meant here by applied "effectively" involves "intention," or motive, far more than "skill." Good skills and manipulative intention will not create long-lasting effectiveness. Poor skills, however, can be overcome by pure, appropriate intention—intention that is nurturing, supportive, and encouraging of our people. Furthermore, over time, good intention will lead naturally to the development of effective skills. The *intention* of leadership, therefore, provides the *key* to making everything we have discussed in this book work. Without a supportive intention of leadership, none of it works.

How does intention show up? Intention shows up in our *being*, in *who we are*. It shows up in our walk, not necessarily in our talk. What or who we really are speaks loudly in our actions. Our gestures, body language, facial expressions, reactions, decisions, attitudes, relations with our people—all these communicate our intention. It is important to link intention to leadership, because the intention of leadership speaks louder than any surface actions or words. Regardless of what is said or done by leadership, people will perceive the real intention behind it.

Let's look at an example of this concept. As discussed, the ultimate or Enlightened Leader has the versatility and "response-ability" to operate up and down the Reactive-Creative Leader continuum and probably spends more than 80% of his or her time in the Creative Leader mode. Looking back at Chapter 11, we see that one of the characteristics Creative Leaders possess is that they are "Listen Oriented." Leaders can *try* to listen or *act* as if they are listening, because that is what they are *supposed to do*. However, true listening is not so much something to do as it is an aspect of the place we come from. Indeed, true listening comes from an intention to hear, and that intention is present when one comes from a place of Creative, Enlightened Leadership. We can be quiet and act as if we are listening—putting forth the *image* of the Creative Leader—and really not be listening at all. Yet, people tend to sense whether someone is listening or not. They can tell if we are trying to *do* some Creative Leader *things* or if we are really coming from the aware, interested, caring, nurturing perspective of the true Creative or Enlightened Leader.

All of this is to say that we must *be* Enlightened Leaders, not act like them. The tools and disciplines of this book work only when we operate from this mature state of being. In fact, this statement is true for all other leadership tools as well. The real key to creating the paradigm shift in our people is for us first to make a shift of our own.

We want our people to shift to a high self-responsibility mode, for this is critical to the renewal of our organization. Yet, they will not make that shift until they feel accepted, trusted, appreciated, and encouraged. Only Enlightened Leaders, through their intention of supporting and developing their people, will send the subtle messages that will generate those positive feelings—and the subsequent shift. To facilitate the shift in the mindset of our people, we must first take full responsibility for our own mindset. We must model the willingness to change ourselves.

BEYOND INDEPENDENCE

Most of the people reading this book have probably been through at least one major stage of renewal in their lives. All of us went through a phase—some only when we were very young, others when we were well into adulthood—when we were very much in the dependency mode. While dependency is natural and healthy when we are infants and small children, it becomes a very limiting state of being later in life. Having our mother make decisions for us early in life is appropriate; depending on her to make decisions for us when we are adults is another matter. At some point it is desirable for us to shift into an independent mode and to making our own decisions. When dependence occurs in adulthood, our personal power is lost and this disempowered state often leads to feeling as though we are victims of circumstances and of other people. Somewhere along our path, however, those who have risen to leadership roles probably experienced a renewal in their lives that moved them out of the dependent, reactive, victim mode and into a more independent, creative, self-responsible one. Such a renewal might or might not have been brought about by a personal crisis.

In this process of renewal, we jumped off onto a new growth curve with self-sufficiency or independence as the primary theme. To make this shift, we threw away our old dependency habits and began to develop different habits that supported our newfound independence. As we developed our independence, we were also developing our self-confidence. Our attitudes shifted substantially as we took more responsibility for our lives. This probably wasn't a digital jump from one end of the Reactive-Creative thinking scale to the other, but it was a clear, substantial, paradigm shift in our mindset. Multiple aspects of our lives were positively impacted. Performance improved in our business life. With the improvement in self-esteem and performance came advancements up the corporate ladder. We took control of our lives and it paid off. It got most of us to the leadership positions in which we find ourselves today. It was a natural part of maturing.

Remember, we are only talking about those people who have already achieved significant leadership roles—people like yourself. Nearly 100% of us in leadership roles have experienced a personal renewal that, in turn, helped us reach a certain level of self-esteem and independence. This was a paradigm shift in our attitudes, our mindset, our perspective. It might have occurred suddenly or very gradually. In either case, it represented major growth for us, and we achieved much satisfaction and many benefits from it.

However, the 80/20 Rule of Thumb probably applies here, and that stage of growth is probably where 80% of us still remain. Many stopped our growth there—in the self-sufficient, independent stage—to remain in its relative comfort and apparent security.

This natural stage of life represents the growth curve from which we must jump to attain the maturity of the Enlightened Leader. Before making the paradigm shift to this new level of enlightened awareness and perspective—a new growth curve, pre-Enlightened Leaders begin to notice the limitations of their independent mindset. While it has served them well in the past, they see that it no longer does so.

In their leadership roles, they recognize that the independent mode is also a control mode. They find they can control, to some extent, the hands and feet of their people, but they cannot access the large amounts of discretionary energy held by their people's hearts and minds. They discover that the control orientation of the independent mode limits their ability to effectively delegate real responsibility and leads to the development of barriers between people and between departments as well. Furthermore, the independent mode of "I can do it better myself" or "Do it my way" certainly does not support the building of trust among our people. It does not support the development of effective, cooperative relationships so critical to ongoing organizational renewal. It also does not support people down in the ranks moving past the dependency mode. In fact it tends to encourage them to stay at that level, which limits their personal performance, growth, and satisfaction.

The characteristics of this independent stage of personal development closely correspond to some of the characteristics of the Reactive Leadership style. Examples include Reactive Leaders' need to have their own answers, their tendency toward a "tell" orientation, their need to make the decisions personally, and their fear of losing control. These characteristics are all related to an independent stage of growth.

The limitations of this personal-growth/Reactive-Leadership style show up organizationally in many ways—disappointing results, resistance to change, discontent among our people, withheld discretionary energy, lack of commitment, poor quality, and negative attitudes. These are all symptoms of the underlying soft issues that occur when leadership operates from a mindset unclear about the criticality of working together, unclear about the importance of supportive relationships among their people. These limitations are being experienced by many organizations all over America today.

When coming from the perspective of the Reactive Leader, or the independent stage of personal growth, we must achieve several difficult shifts before we move into Enlightened Leadership. These are listed below:

We must let go of our ego-driven need to have our own answers. The answers that will work are those from the people who have to make them work. To accomplish this shift, we must first build up our ego (self-confidence) until we no longer need to validate ourselves by having our own answers. At this point, we can be more open and let others contribute at a deeper level.

We must let go of our need for strict control and trust our people. For our people to be self-responsible and empowered, they must be provided with the power and authority to be so. For them to trust us, they must first feel trusted by us. To be able to do this, we must first trust ourselves.

We must drop our need to be right. The ego-driven need to be right has sidetracked many efforts and created barriers between people that are difficult to tear down. This need to be right doesn't allow anyone else to be right; therefore, we make them wrong. When we make them wrong, we foster lower self-esteem and disempower them—both of which sabotage our efforts at renewal. Do we want to be right or do we want to be effective? We have to choose.

We must drop our protective barriers and be open and vulnerable. We must drop the facades and masks we use to protect our perception of who we are, and just *be* who we *really* are. For many leaders, this means being the same person at work as we are *away* from work. We must be a real person to our people. We must be honest with them about who we are.

One hard fact exists: to create the shift in our people, as leaders we must first make our own move toward Enlightened Leadership. This step is not easy, but neither is the shift of our people to a mindset centered on self-responsibility. When we weigh the difficulty of our own change, perhaps we can better understand and remember what our people are going through in their shift—for it is a shift we probably have experienced in the past. If we want to support that transformation in them, we have no choice but to demonstrate a shift ourselves. The only choice we have revolves around time frame—when will we make the shift?

Nearly all of us *can develop* into Enlightened Leaders. It actually represents a normal step in the human maturation process. The innate abilities to be Enlightened Leaders are already within us. We just have to drop our protective barriers, be who we really are, and let those natural abilities surface.

THE ESSENCE OF ENLIGHTENED LEADERSHIP

A much smaller number of leaders, probably fewer than 20%, already have experienced another level of personal renewal. These *are* the Enlightened Leaders.

Enlightened Leaders might or might not have experienced another personal crisis that encouraged them to break out of their limiting boxes and move into renewal. However it happened, they took a hard look at the limitations of their independent mode and found new clarity about the natural laws of nature, which then moved them onto a new growth curve—one that recognizes the *interdependent* nature of mankind.

The full awareness of the true interdependence of people separates Enlightened Leaders from those who are *trying to do* Enlightened Leader *things* or *trying to be* Enlight-

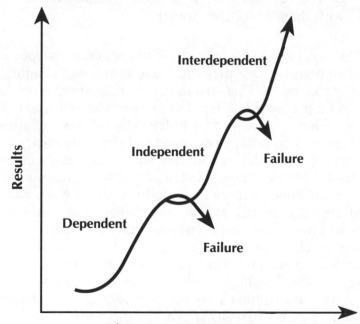

ened Leaders. This is not an intellectual awareness but something they know in their hearts to be true. They know the criticality of working together to provide both optimal effectiveness and personal satisfaction. They understand the link between working well together and enjoying our work.

They know that experiencing joy in what we are doing, which literally represents *the essence* of W. Edwards Deming's lifelong work, is fundamental to ultimate individual and organizational performance. Provide an opportunity and an environment that allows people to enjoy their work while setting high expectations for performance, and watch performance go up. When the performance goes up, so do the self-esteem and job and personal satisfaction, which again positively impacts performance.

Enlightened Leaders know that the hearts and minds of their people can be won when they are working toward a purpose they find worthwhile, are involved in the planning and decision-making, and feel appreciated by leadership. They know that people must feel okay with themselves *as they are* before they will be strong enough to look inside themselves for the possibility of change. They know that enhanced self-image encourages the honest reflection necessary for personal growth. They know, because they have personally experienced both sides of the situation through their own multiple personal renewals.

They have discovered the answers that work for any team are the ones developed by that team itself. Automatic commitment and buy-in for the solution are built in when people solve their own problems. Enlightened Leaders know people will give their all in working *together* to accomplish their *shared* vision. They know the amazing power of numbers when people work together in synergy toward a shared goal.

Enlightened Leaders truly appreciate people and want to help them grow and prosper as individuals. They know their ultimate role is to support their people. They are crystal clear about the awesome power of acceptance of people, and the welfare of their people comes first in their minds. They know that leadership has been responsible for encouraging the disempowering, dependent relationships that probably exist in their organizations, and they take responsibility for supporting their people's shift to independent and interdependent relationships for their benefit as well as for the organization's.

Each leader's personal stage of growth sets the limit for what can be expected of his or her people. People are not likely to grow past where the leader has grown. Therefore, if we want our people to work closely together in synergistic teams, we must come from the honest interdependent mode of the Enlightened Leader. If we show up in the independent mode and try to *do* interdependent things to encourage teamwork, they will see right through us. They will get the message that this is just talk, and we are not really serious about working closely together as teams. We'll get less than or equal to what we model. People are impacted

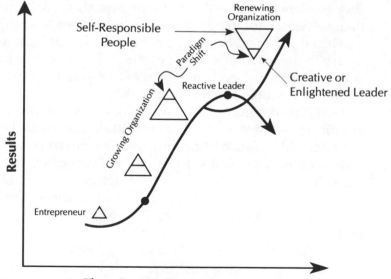

by who or what we are far more than what we do. If we want to build good teams, we had better *be* great team players. Credibility and respect are instantly lost if we try to act like something we are not. Our intention has to be forthright and honest.

THE PERSONAL CHALLENGE

Right now in America the alarm clock is ringing to awaken Enlightened Leadership. Such leaders are sorely needed, and that need will not soon disappear. Yet, we keep hitting the snooze button, thus delaying our choice to waken up and get started. Every time we hit that button, the crisis draws nearer. And if we wait until a major crisis occurs, organizationally or personally, recovery may be difficult or even impossible.

The choice is ours. No one else can make this decision for us. We cannot count on anyone or anything outside of ourselves to do it. When will we be ready? Clearly, we first have to feel good enough about who we are to be willing to take a chance. We have to trust that we will be okay no matter what. We have to be confident enough in the rewards awaiting us that we are willing to take the personal risk to achieve them. It is a significant investment in our lives. We must treat it as such and feel that the return on investment is worth the risk.

When we are ready, when we are strong enough to go out on the limb—where the fruit is—what do we do? Very simply, take action! Move outside our current limiting boxes. Choose a *different* action than we have in the past in an area that is important enough that it feels risky. If there's no feeling of risk, there's little likelihood of reward. The key is to begin; the rest is easy.

As an example of such risk, Ed shares the action that he took to break out of an old box that opened him to personal renewal:

"A major step toward personal renewal that I took involves my father. For many years of my life, I had very little respect for him because of things that happened when I was growing up. All I could see were the things that he did wrong. My focus was clearly on the back side of the 'what's-wrong-what's-right' NeFER.

"While attending a personal-development seminar some years ago, I realized that much of the responsibility for our poor relationship was due to my own negative focus. Though I had considered myself a 'positive' thinker for years, I finally understood that my attitude concerning my father really was *my* choice.

"That led me to consider how few years he might have left to live. Regardless of how I felt about what had happened earlier, I knew that I wanted to have a good relationship with my father.

"Once I comprehended the depth of my choices, I shifted into a more forgiving mode. I realized that forgiveness had nothing to do with him—I was responsible for forgiving.

"I decided to meet with my father. It was April, and I had not seen him since Christmas. I had one objective in mind: no matter what else happened, I wanted to hug my father for the first time since I could remember instead of giving him my usual handshake. I had no idea what else I would do or say, but I was determined to hug him. That was the action I decided to take, and it felt very risky. I was extremely fearful of being rejected, of not having my hug returned by him.

"He met me at the airport. With my heart pounding hard and fast, I walked up to him and ignored his outreached hand. I hugged him. Without hesitation, he hugged me back. It felt wonderful to me, and I could sense that it did for him, too. That one action started washing away years and years of disappointment and hurt.

"From my one commitment—merely to hug him—we moved into a new level of relationship. We spent the entire day together talking like we had never done before. We talked about a lot of things—substantive things—we'd never before discussed. We both agreed it was the best time we had ever spent together.

"When he drove me to the airport the next day, I hugged him again and stepped a little further out on the limb. . . . I said, 'I love you, Dad.' He said, 'I love you, too, Ed.' That was a first! It was a very emotional experience for me.

"Our relationship changed dramatically from that event. I like to jokingly tell people how amazed I was at how much *he* had changed between Christmas and April. Of course, we know who *really* changed.

"Our relationship continued to warm all because I took responsibility for taking the first action that was completely outside the box I had been living in for so many years. I changed *my* attitude about my father—a shift in mindset from being quite reactive to being more creative. Instead of being stuck in only noticing what was wrong with my father, I now began to notice what was right with him. And I saw a *lot* right! The more our relationship was renewed, the more I came to appreciate who he was, how much he had done for me, and how much I cared about him.

"I do not know whether my paradigm shift occurred before, during, or after the event itself, but the conscious choice to take action outside my current box and the action .itself provided the keys to unlock my ability to shift. The personal renewal I experienced from that action impacted all aspects of my life in remarkable ways. I feel that I launched off on a brand-new personal growth curve, and the benefits showed up everywhere.

"For example, the empowerment I felt from this one experience led me to an action that had a dramatic impact on my growth in the business world. It was the scariest, riskiest thing I had ever done as a manager," Ed claims.

Remember the story we told in Chapter 5 about the sales vice president who held a critical meeting with his 250 people. There are two aspects of the event that we have not shared. First, that sales vice president was Ed. Second, he did *not* open the meeting with positive statements about the company's last six months.

Imagine the scenario once again: There were 250 upset and anxious people present. Having experienced two lay-offs, poor sales trends, and numerous other problems, they were understandably concerned about their future with this company. In addition, many of them were late arriving in this western city and angry and upset, because the hotel was slow in checking them in, thus forcing them to wait until after their meetings to check into their rooms. While some were wondering who would be laid off next, others were ready to quit.

Despite the tension and emotions, having an empowering, productive meeting was crucial to the renewal of the sales organization and the entire company. To be successful, *everyone* had to be fully involved and focused on a positive outcome.

Ed tells the rest of the story this way: "The encouragement I had gained from taking the risk with my father helped me to take one of the most interdependent actions I had ever taken as a manager. Instead of telling this hostile audience about the positive things that had occurred over the last six months, *I asked them!* After a very brief introduction, I asked, 'What are the positive things—no matter how small or large—that have happened? What are the successes we have had in our company in the last six months?'

"There was absolute silence. You could have heard the proverbial pin drop. I was petrified about what might or might not happen. It seemed like an eternity, but probably thirty seconds of silence passed before one person finally raised her hand. She shared a simple success that someone in her office had enjoyed. We wrote it on a flip chart. I gained a little bit of hope but was still quite nervous.

"Another ten seconds probably passed before someone else raised his hand with something positive to share. While we were writing this one on the flip chart, two other people raised their hands. Then a handful of hands, then a dozen or so. Before we knew what was happening, the encouraging responses mushroomed. Within five minutes of the original question, we were writing the inputs on two flip charts as fast as we could. The energy in the room was rising dramatically. You could feel the change occurring. The positive emotion was contagious and completely overwhelmed the original tension.

"A dramatic, paradigm shift in the attitudes of the people in that room occurred within fifteen minutes of beginning the meeting in that 'risky' manner. At the end of my so-called presentation, I received a standing ovation. I was personally overwhelmed with emotion, and the president of the company, who was sitting in the back of the room, was in tears. What a validation for me about interdependence.

"Over the following two days, the management team continued asking Effective Questions and focusing all that unleashed energy of empowerment on what needed to be done to affect positive change. That meeting was, indeed, the key to turning the momentum of the organization around. It was a renewal for many people—especially for me."

When we take that first step and we give it our best effort, we will be rewarded—maybe richly rewarded, maybe only somewhat but enough to encourage us to take another step out on the limb. As we take additional steps, the positive reinforcement we need to keep us going accelerates. Before we know it—whoosh!—we have experienced a paradigm shift that has taken us to a new level of being, a brand-new growth curve—the exciting mode of the Enlightened Leader, the leader who truly works *with* people *interdependently.*

A SELF-APPRAISAL

We would like to wrap up this book by encouraging you to take a few minutes to do some personal reflection. For your own benefit and perhaps that of your family, friends, team, and organization, please give thoughtful attention to the following exercise. We encourage you to write down your responses or discuss them with someone who is important and close to you. You might even invite your entire team to do the exercise at the same time. It is a powerful way to prepare for jointly developing a shared team vision.

One beneficial way to address these questions might be to write down or discuss all the thoughts you initially have about them—right now. Then continue to reflect on them and come back to supplement your initial thoughts in a day or two.

The questions in this exercise are intended to support you in gaining clarity about where you are in your own life and in your role as a leader. Your responses will serve as a reminder of what is important to you and what you really care about. In addition, the exercise is designed to help you reclarify where you want to go with your life and with your role as a leader. The deeper the clarity of this vision or image, the more valuable and supportive it will be to your continuing growth and renewal as a person and leader. Consequently, you might want to repeat the exercise periodically, perhaps two or three times a year.

Only when we are clear about what we want, what is important to us, can we make effective, conscious choices that lead us toward our goals. So let's go well out into the future to the end of your life and determine how it turned out. Yes, we want to imagine what it would be like to look back at your life once it is too late to do anything about it.

Specifically, imagine your own funeral where all the people who are important to you or to whom you are important are gathered—your family, friends, and business associates. They are all there to honor you, and you have a special opportunity to address the gathering by way of an audio tape you prepared in advance. This is your chance to review the different aspects of your life as you lived it in detail. This is your occasion to celebrate your life.

Here are some questions to guide you in writing that address:

1. Imagining the end of your life, in as much
   detail as possible, what would you want to be
   able to say at your own funeral about who you
   are and what you have done that you were
   most proud of:
   - **with regard to your family?** *He Cared / Gave of himself*
   - **with regard to your friends?** *Good Person / Generous*
   - **with regard to your business peers?** *Honest / Fair / Helped Smart*
   - **with regard to those who are in the organi-
     zation you led?**

   How would you like to be able to describe your life
   in each of its aspects such that you would have
   absolutely no regrets or disappointments?

   Please thoroughly complete this part before
   continuing.

2. Shifting perspectives, if your life suddenly
   ended tomorrow, what would you be able to
   say truthfully *right now* about who you are
   and what you have done in your life that you
   are most proud of:
   - **with regard to your family?** *Loyal*
   - **with regard to your friends?**
   - **with regard to your business peers?**
   - **with regard to those who are in the organi-
     zation you led?**

3. What specific actions could you take immediately to begin filling the gap between what
   you would *like* to be able to say about your life
   and what you would honestly *have* to say about
   it today:
   - **with regard to your family?**
   - **with regard to your friends?**
   - **with regard to your business peers?**

- **with regard to those who are in the organization you led?**

Just as you and your people have the ability to discover all the solutions you will ever need for organizational issues, *you* personally have access to all the solutions you will ever need for your own life and leadership issues. The key to accessing them is found in asking yourself the right questions and *listening*.

Truthfully, the key to your organization's renewal is you. It has to start with you. The choice to implement what you know is yours. The time is now. What action will you take today to become even more of an Enlightened Leader?

Change-Friendly Highlights

1. A supportive intention is the critical ingredient that must be present for these renewal tools, disciplines, and framework to work.

2. To encourage change in others, leaders must model their own willingness to change.

3. Most people in leadership roles today have likely developed a high level of self-sufficiency and independence.

4. To move to a new level of personal development and leadership effectiveness, independent leaders must undergo another stage of renewal—they must move to the *interdependent* stage.

5. To stimulate this natural maturity process, leaders must take a risk and *take action* outside their limiting "independent" boxes.

6. The key to the renewal of our people, thus the renewal of our organization, is our own *self*-renewal.

We must be the change we wish to see in the world.

MAHATMA GANDHI

BIBLIOGRAPHY

Altany, David, "Lead Now or Forever Rest in Peace," *Industry Week*, April 17, 1989.

Barker, Joel Arthur, *Discovering the Future: The Business of Paradigms* (St. Paul: ILI Press, 1988).

Bennis, Warren, *On Becoming a Leader* (Addison-Wesley, 1989).

Bennis, Warren, and Bert Nanus, *Leaders: The Strategies for Taking Charge* (New York: Harper & Row, 1985).

Block, Peter, *The Empowered Manager* (Jossey-Bass, 1988).

Covey, Stephen, *The Seven Habits of Highly Effective People* (New York: Simon & Schuster, 1990).

Crum, Thomas S., *The Magic of Conflict* (New York: Simon & Schuster, 1987).

Drucker, Peter F., *The New Realities* (New York: Harper & Row, 1989).

Gerber, Michael E., *The E Myth: Why Most Businesses Don't Work and What to Do About It* (Cambridge MA: Ballinger Publishing Company).

Goldratt, Eliyahu, and Jeff Cox, *The Goal: A Process of Ongoing Improvement* (New York: North River Press, 1986).

Hagberg, Janet, *Real Power* (Minneapolis: Winston Press, 1984).

Hawken, Paul, *Growing a Business* (New York: Simon & Schuster, 1987).

Helmstetter, Shad, Ph.D., *What to Say When You Talk to Yourself* (New York: Simon & Schuster, 1986).

Iacocca, Lee, with Sonny Kleinfield, *Talking Straight* (New York: Bantam Books, 1988).

Kouzes, James M., and Barry Z. Posner, *The Leadership Challenge: How to Get Extraordinary Things Done in Organizations* (Josse-Bass, 1987).

Larson, Carl E., and Frank M. J. LaFasto, *Teamwork: What*

Must Go Right, What Can Go Wrong (Newbury Park, CA: Sage Publications, 1989).

Lynch, Dudley, and Paul Kordis, *Strategy of the Dolphin: Scoring a Win in a Chaotic World* (New York: William Morrow, 1988).

Mayer, Richard J., *Conflict Management: The Courage to Confront* (Columbus, OH: Battelle Press, 1990).

Miller, Lawrence M., *American Spirit: Visions of a New Corporate Culture* (New York: William Morrow, 1984).

Miller, Lawrence M., *Barbarians to Bureaucrats: Corporate Life Cycle Strategies* (New York: Clarkson N. Potter, 1989).

Naisbitt, John, and Patricia Aburdene, *Megatrends 2000: Ten New Directions for the 1990s* (New York: Avon Books, 1990).

Nulty, Peter, *"The Soul of an Old Machine,"* Fortune Magazine, May 21, 1990.

Peck, M. Scott, *The Road Less Traveled* (New York: Simon & Schuster, 1978).

Peters, Tom, *Thriving on Chaos: Handbook for a Management Revolution* (New York: Harper & Row, 1987).

Schaef, Anne Wilson, and Diane Fassel, *The Addictive Organization* (San Francisco: Harper & Row, 1988).

Walton, Mary, *The Deming Management Method* (New York: Perigee Books, 1986).

Waterman, Robert H., Jr., *The Renewal Factor* (New York: Bantam Books, 1987).

Wilson, Larry, *Changing the Game: The New Way to Sell* (New York: Simon & Schuster, 1987).

Yankelovich, Daniel, "Our Turn," *American Health*, September 1988.

INDEX

ABOUT ENLIGHTENED LEADERSHIP INTERNATIONAL, INC

At the heart of every person and organization is the desire to make the world a better place. Enlightened Leadership International is dedicated to doing just that, to creating an environment that brings out the best in individuals as well as in the organizations where they work.

Enlightened Leadership workshops create lasting transformation. The workshops actually generate a paradigm shift in how people perceive themselves, their work, and each other. This shift in attitudes is often described by our clients as the vital missing piece in most improvement methods today. We at Enlightened Leadership International hold a simple belief:

An organization's people already have the solutions to virtually every challenge they face; the issue is how to access those solutions.

To receive your complimentary copies of our writings on contemporary leadership issues or to order
Enlightened Leadership, call:
(800) 798-9881
These articles include: "Quality: The Human Factor,"
"Team Health Indicators,"
"The Missing Piece in TQM," or "Enlightened Leadership: The Heart of Quality"

For additional information regarding all the services available through Enlightened Leadership International, Inc., contact:

Enlightened Leadership International, Inc.
7100 East Belleview Avenue, Suite G11
Englewood, CO 80111–1632
(800) 798-9881
(303) 694-4644
FAX (303) 694-4705   *Enlightened Leadership International*

From all of us of the Enlightened Leadership Team, we want to thank you for reaching out to the Enlightened Leader in you! Each of us can make a positive difference in this world.